Life Lines

FORREST CHURCH

Life Lines

Holding On *(and Letting Go)*

Beacon Press · Boston

Beacon Press
25 Beacon Street
Boston, Massachusetts 02108-2892
www.beacon.org

Beacon Press books are published under the auspices of
the Unitarian Universalist Association of Congregations.

11 10 09 08   10 9 8 7

Text design by Christopher Kuntze
Composition by Wilsted & Taylor

This book is printed on acid-free paper that meets the uncoated paper ANSI/NISO
specifications for permanence as revised in 1992.

Library of Congress Cataloging-in-Publication Data can be found on page 172.

The excerpt of "Easter Sunday, 1955," by Elizabeth Spires is from *Worlding* by
Elizabeth Spires, copyright ©1995 by Elizabeth Spires, and is reprinted by
permission of W. W. Norton & Company, Inc.

To Carolyn

"Anyone who is linked with all that live
still has some hope."

Contents

Acknowledgments

Four years ago, having completed a book on theology and politics, I found myself drawn to more intimate questions, matters of personal spirituality. Responding to my parishioners' growing hunger for spiritual connections, I also felt an inner need for lifelines to sustain me in my own journey. After several false starts, I enlisted aid from two wonderful sources: the wise old preacher in Ecclesiastes and my friends. Together, they helped me clarify and shape my thoughts into their present form.

This book would not have been possible without the confidence and criticism of Wendy Strothman, now executive vice president at Houghton Mifflin, who accepted my inchoate initial proposal on faith and then rejected, gently but firmly, several really quite embarrassing drafts. When Wendy moved from her position as publisher and editor in chief of Beacon Press, my present editor, Susan Worst, took up the slack. In all my years as a

Acknowledgments

writer, I have never received better or more detailed editorial advice than Wendy and Susan offered me.

Neither they nor several others who read numerous vagrant drafts are responsible for the imperfections that remain, but without their counsel this book would be almost unrecognizably different. Among the many friends and colleagues who have helped me, I owe special gratitude to Steven Bauman, Ken Beldon, Debra Berger, Robert Birge, June Bingham Birge, Robert Brawer, Minna Buck, Bill Coffin, Annie Gorycki, Galen Guengerich, Holly Hendrix, Richard Leonard, Nick Limansky, Barbara Merritt, Joe Miller, Wayne Rood, and Tony Schwartz.

In addition, I am profoundly indebted to my parishioners of the past two decades, the people of All Souls Church in New York City, as bighearted a congregation as I can possibly imagine.

I dedicate this book to my wife, Carolyn Buck Luce. Her empathy, compassion, and unconditional love have taught me volumes. She is my lifeline.

New Year's Day, 1996
All Souls Church
New York City

Introduction

Five years ago, on the first Sunday of Lent, I found the following anonymous letter tucked under the door of my minister's study.

Dear Mr. Church,

What is the meaning of adversity? I don't think I can handle it anymore. Nothing it seems has gone right in my life. I am very tired of this stupid life. If you can tell me the reason for suffering or pain or adversity, please tell me. I know people do not have an answer, and I know many people overcome adversity but I am tired of it. I feel absolutely hopeless. Is there a god or is there not a god? If I feel there is not a god what is the sense of going on? And for whom?

I know this letter sounds crazy, but I am tired of it. I feel absolutely hopeless.

A parishioner

P.S. Yes, I've had therapy and medication—now you must really think I'm crazy—but I remain hopeless. Please help me.

The next morning, I set out to identify the anonymous, apparently suicidal parishioner who had slipped
this heartrending note under my door. All Souls Church
is relatively large, but I can match many faces with names.
Through my counseling and the grapevine that winds up
the walls of every community, I harbored some confidence that, with the help of my staff, I could somehow
identify this individual. We sorted through the people we
felt at greatest risk and made a few discreet calls. But we
didn't find the person we were looking for. That's because
we were looking for a piece of hay in a haystack. I should
have known it without thinking. Any member of my congregation could have written that letter.

He could be the shy man whose name I do not know,
who sits in the last pew and leaves right before the benediction. She could be the unemployed teacher with cancer; the single mother with two hyperactive children; the
accountant with a gambling problem who just declared
bankruptcy; or the homeless man, once a successful
banker, who can't seem to stay on his medication. But just
as likely she could be the successful Wall Street analyst or
the big corporate lawyer with the stunning family. He
could be the starring Broadway actor or the boy who inherited ten million dollars and now is a man. When it
comes to despair, playing odds according to looks or fortune is a fool's game. In Edwin Arlington Robinson's
poem it is Richard Cory, the mogul, not one of his oppressed workers, who goes out one night and puts a bullet
through his head.

During twenty years as a pastoral counselor, I have

seen people hold on for dear life through every manner of personal crisis. It is humbling to be asked to assist another who is in pain. Often crises that other people struggle to endure, I can hardly imagine enduring myself. Sometimes they succumb. Sometimes they survive. In both cases, I have witnessed—and this is perhaps the greatest privilege of ministry—remarkable displays of human courage and resilience. I have witnessed something else as well, the thing that inspired me to write this book. Surprisingly often, my parishioners emerge from their struggles not only intact but with a more profound appreciation for life's meaning. The same trial that destroys one person can actually strengthen another.

Over the years, my parishioners have taught me two lessons. When cast into the depths, to survive we must first let go of things that will not save us. Then we must reach out for things that can. As to the former, until we free ourselves from an attachment to false sources of security and let go of our illusions, we will remain in the abyss. With respect to the latter, the most important thing to remember is that lifelines have two ends. To grasp one end, however tightly, avails us nothing unless the other end is secured. Unless we reach out to and for others, seeking meaning not in our own suffering but in our shared experience of the human condition, our lifelines will not hold.

I still don't know "the meaning of adversity." Nor do I know "the reason for suffering or pain." These are intractable questions. But if intractable questions cannot be answered, difficult questions often can.

How can we make peace with our mortality and the death of those we love? How can we accept things that cannot be changed and change the things that can? How can we forgive ourselves and others? How can we gather the courage to overcome our fears? How can we connect with others to fashion a more just society, a more loving community? And where can we find God in what may seem at times a godless world? Not to mention one of the questions my anonymous parishioner grew tired of asking. It is a good question and can be answered. How is it that some people manage to conquer adversity, while others are consumed by it?

I shall explore these questions in the following pages. To test the validity of my answers, the criterion I suggest is simple. If life does hold meaning, accessibility to this meaning must be universal, the answers meaningful to everyone. This may seem obvious, but any quest for meaning that doesn't begin with the obvious is more likely to prove fanciful than illuminating.

This said, my thesis is a simple one, no different really from the ancient philosophy presented in the Book of Ecclesiastes. In the Hebrew scriptures, Ecclesiastes is numbered among the wisdom books, or Megilloth. As distinguished from the Torah (the first five books of the Bible, which contain the law), the books of history (which tell the story of the kingdoms of Israel and Judah), and the writings of the prophets, the wisdom literature addresses questions of morality and meaning. More a work of philosophy than theology and so universalistic in tone that it stands apart somewhat from the other writings in the

Hebrew canon, Ecclesiastes suggests that life is difficult, fragile, painful, unpredictable, unfathomable, and limited.

Simply put, everyone suffers. That is a given. Suffering is a birthright far more inalienable than happiness. And the shares are not allotted evenly. We need not look far to find evidence for this. How often innocents, especially children, seem to suffer an unequal, undeserved share of affliction. Since neither justice nor injustice is distributed proportionally, life is anything but fair. Not only does the rain fall but the sun also shines on both the just and the unjust. Just try to make sense of it. "I have seen everything that is done under the sun," the Preacher writes, "and behold, all is vanity and a striving after wind."

Yet all is not hopeless. Despite our ignorance and suffering, hope emerges in the lifelines that connect us. The Preacher begins by finding meaning in our common fate. "The right happiness for men and women is to eat and drink and be content with all the work we have to do under the sun, during the few days God has given us to live, since this is the lot assigned to all of us." He then turns to the ways in which we can serve one another. We should not hoard our bread but "cast it upon the waters." We should "give a portion to seven and also to eight." "Two are better than one," he says, . . . "for if they fall, the one will lift up his or her neighbor, but woe to those who are alone when they fall, for they have no one to help them up."

Everyone suffers, but not everyone despairs. Despair is a consequence of suffering only when affliction cuts us off from others. It need not. The same suffering that leads one person to lose all hope can as easily promote empathy, a felt appreciation for other people's pain. Grief, failure, even death, can thus be sacraments. Not that suffering is valuable in and of itself. As my anonymous parishioner's letter so eloquently demonstrates, if one suffers alone, suffering is no elixir. A sacrament symbolizes communion, the act of bringing us together. Suffering brings us together when we discover the lifelines that connect our hearts.

In the following pages, I offer a loosely orchestrated set of variations on the above themes. Drawing freely from Ecclesiastes (itself freely drawn), other like religious teachings, my own life, and the lives of my parishioners, my goal is to render life's shadows—suffering, loss, failure, cosmic ignorance—as honestly as possible, even as I seek meaning within and between them. I shall open with the interplay of love and death, follow this with a search for self-acceptance and forgiveness, and then explore the dual promise of humility and compassion, each a lifeline connecting us to God and one another. To close, I shall revisit these themes in search of honest hope, the kind of hope that sustains us when life turns bad but also awakens us from taking our lives for granted, from begrudging what we cannot explain or slighting what is ours to cherish.

I still haven't identified my anonymous parishioner, but the letter tucked under my study door four years ago has never been far from my mind. With appreciation for the pain and courage it represents, here is my answer.

PART I

Love & Death:
Lifelines to the Heart

"The living know at least that they will die."

ECCLESIASTES 9:5

When I was a little boy, my Presbyterian grandmother taught me a bedtime prayer. "God bless Mommy. God bless Daddy. And you, Mom Mom, and Pop Pop, and Brownie [my monkey]," and—to postpone the inevitable—as many more blessings as I could tack to a single litany: Lala and Smoky. Chris, Jimmy. My goldfish. The sun and the moon.

"That's enough, dear."

Like millions of other children, to close my prayer I would then repeat words once passed down to her and to her parents before her: "If I should die before I wake, I pray the Lord my soul to take."

Gently my grandmother would smooth and kiss my forehead. "Sleep tight, dear. Don't let the bedbugs bite."

3

What a curious notion of comfort, to haunt children to sleep, interjecting specters of death and biting insects. I wasn't haunted, of course; I was lulled, in the spirit of that famous lullaby:

> *"Rockaby baby, in the treetop.*
> *When the wind blows, the cradle will rock.*
> *When the bough breaks, the cradle will fall,*
> *And down will come baby, cradle and all."*

It's difficult to imagine a panel of modern child care professionals stamping its seal of approval on this ancient verse or on the prayer my grandmother taught me, not to mention her playful goodnight warning. Yet, something deep is at work here. The coupling of night and sleep with death and danger is not accidental. These old-fashioned bedtime runes spring from a time when death and danger were embraced as so intrinsic to human experience that parents unself-consciously prepared themselves and their children for them every sundown. In this respect, the words do carry an implicit powerful message. By definition, life is precarious. The most protective mother, cradling her child, sometimes cannot prevent the bough from breaking. No matter how hard they try, or how often they are reminded, sleeping children cannot keep bedbugs from biting. And when, like a thief in the night, death pays a visit, we cannot pray that the door be bolted or the window shuttered, only that the Lord may keep our soul.

Today, when I say my night-time prayers, I take a few deep breaths to quiet my thoughts. I conduct an inventory of my day. I confess, forgive, try to remember to give thanks. But then, rather than drifting off to sleep, I sometimes lie awake, restless, anxious about the morrow. The bedbugs in my psyche bite. Death may even haunt. I wish I could undo things I have done or had done something I should have. Sometimes when this happens I think of my grandmother and invert the childhood prayer she taught me. What would it mean, if I should wake before I die?

This is a religious question. Religion is our human response to the dual reality of being alive and having to die. We are not the animal with tools or the animal with language, we are the religious animal. We know that we must die, and therefore we question what life means. Reflecting back on my grandmother and her simple faith, I sense that many of us today have lost something precious. Not dogma, not a rule book, but a sense of life that *did* know death, that accepted all-too-human as human enough, and led to a reconciliation of human being with human love, weakness, failure, and loss.

My grandmother was remarkably ordinary, by no means a saint or a sage. She knew her share of suffering, but it was essential to her worldview. An upbringing in relative poverty. The loss of her first child. A near fatal illness as a young woman, with a long convalescence. In many ways, her life was hard. Yet my grandmother appeared to have found something we all seek. She had made peace with life. She didn't demand more than life was likely to offer. I can't imagine her ever confusing wisdom with knowledge. As long as everyone in the family had more to eat than they wanted and the weather cooperated with her plans, she seemed fully content. When her plans were thwarted, she accepted that too. In no sense conspicuously pious, she never preached and rarely judged another, at least not openly. She took life as it came and died at the age of ninety-six.

I remember her nursing her father at home as he lay dying. I remember her knitting through the pain of her own acute arthritis and helping her drug-addicted sister make it from bed to table. I remember her teaching me to pray. What I don't remember is her ever complaining that life was unfair.

I admit I romanticize my grandmother. Though she lived until I was thirty-five, I never really knew her thoughts or fears. Accepting her lot as a caregiver, without ambitions beyond those assigned to most women of her time, she displayed a passivity that I may have confused with contentment. Given how strong she seemed and yet how quiet she was, I expect that she might have been a very different woman had she come of age today. Yet, my grandmother did appear to have understood one important thing about life that many of us resist acknowledging. She seems never to have questioned that life, by definition, is a struggle, with suffering its frequent cost and death its final price.

"The heart of the wise
is in the house of mourning."

ECCLESIASTES 7:5

I have attended funeral receptions, even wakes, where any subject save death and the departed loved one seemed permissible. When grandparents, parents, even children died at home, death was an inescapable presence in our lives. Today, shielded from intimacy with death by the cold, mechanically invasive, and antiseptic chambers of hospitals, we not only escape the full brunt of its mysterious and forbidding presence, but even more detrimentally, we lose touch with how natural death is.

Frustrating our search for shared meaning, death is also the one subject we are most eager to repress. Sex, religion, and politics once constituted the trinity of taboos that proper people didn't dare broach at a dinner party. Today all three are served up as hors d'oeuvres, titillating tidbits for even the most polite company. The new ta-

7

boos are ones our less insulated if more demure ancestors could not avoid, death and grief. Intrude either into conversation, even among family and friends, and don't be surprised if an awkward silence descends on the company. Two of the experiences that unite us all we avoid mentioning at almost any cost.

I didn't become a minister in any meaningful sense until I conducted my first funeral. Of all the things I am called on to do, none is more important, and none has proved of greater value to me, than the call to be with people at times of loss. When asked at a gathering of colleagues what gives most meaning to my work, I replied that, above all else, it is the constant reminder of death. Death awakens me to life's preciousness and also its fragility.

How often this happens. My desk and mind may be littered with a hundred tasks and grievances. Then death or the threat of dying comes calling at my door. All of a sudden, like a bracing wind it clears my being of all pettiness. It connects me to others. It renews my perspective on life's real joy and pain. This is death's hard gift to me. Not only does it justify my work, it can make me whole again.

Regardless of faith or creed, in this we are all companions ("those who break bread with one another"). In a spiritual rather than material sense, the ultimate bread we mortals break is the bread of life and death.

8

"Much wisdom, much grief;
the more knowledge, the more sorrow."

Let me tell you a story.

Once upon a time a man and woman lived together in a garden. It was paradise: fruit-bearing trees in abundance; perfect weather; nothing to do but frolic naked without shame, perhaps bathe in the bubbling brook or loll in the shade, naming an occasional animal. No appointments to keep, no tasks to fulfill, no bodily pains, no fear of death for there was no death, not even any rules, save one: God forbade the man and woman to eat fruit from the tree of the knowledge of good and evil.

One day a serpent sidled up to the woman. "Eve," it said, "you're being foolish. God told you to keep clear of that tree because the old scoundrel wants to make sure that you never grow up. The moment you bite into that fruit your eyes shall be opened; you will be God's equal, blessed with the knowledge of good and evil."

9

Persuaded by the serpent, Eve talked to Adam and they decided to give knowledge a try. It turned out that the serpent had spoken truth, but not the whole truth. As promised, they became as gods, knowing good and evil. However, God had tucked away a wild card. When Adam and Eve drew knowledge, God trumped it with death.

Immortality and knowledge are what make gods divine. As the story reads, before the fall we were godlike in immortality but not in knowledge. In human terms, the knowledge of good and evil represents not the mastery of cosmic secrets but the kindling of conscience. This is what Adam and Eve purchased at the price of death, inheriting the burdens of a mortal span. Adam must sweat among the thorns and thistles of the field, Eve labor in delivering children. Both are sentenced to return at the end of their days to the dust from which they came.

Before I continue with this story, a word about the Bible. There is no more human book. A panorama of our strivings and longings, howsoever vain, is painted across its magnificent screen. This story does not preach easily. Whatever meaning we discern from the Bible's pages must reckon with Jacob stealing his patrimony from Esau, with King David sending the husband of his mistress to certain death, with God's chosen people suffering one crippling loss after another. But that's why I love the Bible. It reminds me of the world. From the tangible sensuality of the Song of Songs to the cries of Job, from the fall to the crucifixion, the Bible tells the all-too-human story of succeeding generations struggling to wrench meaning from life and death.

The authors of the scriptures did not share, in fact had not even developed, our modern notion of individualism. In the Hebrew Bible, the word "individual" does not appear, for no concept existed to match it. Individualism as we know it only began to flower in the fourth century of the common era, with St. Augustine's *Confessions* the foundational text. With its emphasis on shared rather than individual meaning, ancient religious wisdom is accordingly more universal in scope than much of the spiritual wisdom offered today. Jesus points the way here. When asked to explain how he, a rabbi, could dare break long-established religious rules such as the injunction to honor the Sabbath, he replied that all the law and the prophets can be summed up in two great commandments: to love God and to love our neighbor. Far more universal in temper and scope than most of his followers, Jesus was decidedly *not* a Biblical literalist.

Those who insist on narrow definitions of "God" and "neighbor" in any single creed or set of religious beliefs do so at their neighbor's peril. Any answer to the question, "What does life mean?" that pops up in history after millions of people have already been born and died, any specific solution limited by time or geography and therefore unavailable to those who lived their entire human span without access to it, is a parochial answer. Socrates could not be saved by Jesus. The Buddha could not find enlightenment by meditating on the teachings of the Koran. Truth fills the pages of the Bible and Koran, but it extends beyond those pages. To the extent that it can be discovered, the meaning of mortal existence must be accessible to every human who ever has or ever will live and die. Meaning can be sought and found by people of faith, whatever their faith may be, but a deeper meaning emerges only from what every mortal shares. We don't hold Jesus or Buddha, the Koran or the Rig Veda in common; what unites us is birth and death.

This said, as the ur-legend, or primary explanation for the human condition in Judaism, Christianity, and Islam, the story of the fall as reported in the first two chapters of Genesis is as weighty as any in the entire human canon. Mark how it defines the human lot: a brief, hard existence characterized by labor and suffering that ends in death. That, according to Genesis, is our birthright. Nothing here, at least not yet, about love. Nothing about reunion with God or salvation. And certainly nothing about the right of happiness with which we presumably were endowed by our creator. God's proclamation reads, "To the woman Eve God said: 'I will increase your labor and your groaning, and in labor you shall bear children.' To the man Adam God said: 'Accursed be the ground on your account. With labor you shall win food from it all the days of your life. It will grow thorns and thistles for you, none but wild plants for you to eat. You shall gain your bread by the sweat of your brow until you return to the ground, for from it you were taken. Dust you are, to dust you shall return.'" According to Genesis, affliction is not a pathology of the human condition but its very essence. It is not something we can avoid simply by living right or thinking right; it comes with the territory.

We even enter the world in pain (our mother's pain), through the excruciating passage of childbirth. Here agony issues in victory; pain is instantly redeemed by the ongoing miracle of new creation. Lesser physical pains may be harder to justify, but when considering the heart's anguish that can give birth to a new creation within, we can take some solace in knowing that in childbirth joy is only temporarily veiled by perhaps the greatest physical pain of all.

We may share our mother's pain at birth, in our case the pain of light, the force of hands wrenching us from the familiar, warm comfort of the womb. As long as we are fortunate enough to be born free from hunger, abuse, or disease, we toss this pain off quickly, like a caul, an unneeded garment. Then for a time, everything is an extension of our own being. We take for granted the life force that animates and sustains us. Only as we grow through the pains of separation and ego development do we become involved in the complexities of the human condition. Even then we may continue taking life for granted. Lacking some kind of religious second birth, often precipitated by a crisis in our lives, we may travel in half-conscious flight from death all the way to the grave.

In the fall from Eden, pain and suffering are the keys to wisdom. This motif appears in many traditions, almost always double-edged. First, mortal experience leads to pain, then pain to wisdom. This story also introduces the question of blame. Adam accuses Eve, holding her responsible. In turn, Eve fingers the serpent. Genesis two is chapter one in the history of victimization. Finally, the fall tells the tale of the birth of human willfulness, with separation from God its consequence. Willfulness springs from the strength of our desires. Giving them full rein leads to hubris, or pride. Whether here, in Greek tragedy, or contemporary experience, when we lift ourselves above the law of God or nature's law (however arbitrary such laws may seem), when we ourselves become as gods, we face the consequence of nemesis. In Christian theology, willfulness is the active state of being in sin. Relying only on our own devices rather than ceding control and accepting forgiveness, we exclude the opportunity for redemption.

In Eden, Adam and Eve flourished in a permanent state of infancy. Lacking conscience and consciousness they subsisted, free of pain. In this sense, infancy is our own Eden. As we grow older we may or may not suffer anything as dramatic as the original fall. But all of us fail. No life is free from affliction and grief. When we are cast from the garden into the wilderness, as were Adam and Eve in the second chapter of Genesis, we begin our spiritual journey in earnest. Our search for meaning opens with the awakening of consciousness, in this case the consciousness that we are fated to die. We leave a world of illusion and enter one of shared suffering.

When we first enter this new world, more often than not we do so unwillingly. Cast from the delights of the garden, even from the contentment of semi-consciousness, we fall into the abyss. As we fall, our faith may completely disappear. Yet these moments can constitute the most powerful religious encounters of our lives. Even in God's absence we are confronted by something awful—in both senses of the word—terrible and charged with awe. Such encounters are filled with danger, but also with passion, for we have entered the realm of the holy. Rudolf Otto, in his book *The Idea of the Holy*, defined holy with two Latin words, *tremens et fascinans*: tremendous, a word whose root meaning is fear, and fascinating.

This is both a blessing and a curse. It is a curse, because it is painful. It is a blessing, because so long as we are only half alive, half awake, and hermetically sealed from death, our religion will not be tremendous and fascinating, merely comfortable. The holy will be excluded from our precincts. When we enter the depth dimension, however unbidden, all this changes. We become vulnerable, and God enters through the wounds. Or we ache with the absence of God. Either way, we are temporarily awake, alive. We tremble with an awareness of our mortality.

In life, heights and depths come in pairs. The more we love, the more we risk both pain and loss. The higher we climb, the farther we dare to fall. Put in terms of God, when we need God most, often we can only reach the holy by first encountering the absence of God. By entering the woods. By falling from the wire. By diving into dark, cold waters. Yet, whether we know it or not, our darkest hours and most painful moments unlock the heart's wisdom. Affliction precedes empathy. In both existential and essential terms—in shared experience and in recognition of our common nature—we cannot truly feel another's pain until we have experienced our own.

When Adam and Eve were cast from the garden, God didn't abandon them, they abandoned God. By the same token, when we find ourselves cast into the wilderness or are lost in the woods, it is not a Godforsaken land through which we journey, only one in which wisdom is born of suffering and pain. In a very real sense, as long as Adam and Eve remained in the garden, they didn't need God. Only after they received the consciousness of good and evil, experienced pain, and confronted the inevitability of death did they need God and one another.

Our own lives are no different. When things go well we splash along happily or unconsciously in the shallows. Relying on powers within our control, blissfully inattentive to our mortality and that of our loved ones, self-satisfied and therefore self-contained, all we need to believe in is ourselves. The Persian mystic Rūmī captures this paradox brilliantly. "The servant of God complains to God of pain. He makes a hundred complaints of his pain. God says, 'After all, grief and pain have made thee humbly entreating, and righteous. Make this complaint of bounty and happiness that befalls thee and removes you far from my door, and makes you an outcast.'" Or as the old adage puts it, "Our extremity is God's opportunity."

On a superficial level, such a reading trivializes God into a bully who hurts us in order to evoke our respect. Though this interpretation could be teased from certain passages in the Bible (including the first two chapters of Genesis), the more important lesson, one which appears throughout the scriptures, is that we cannot save ourselves. Accordingly, we are at greatest peril when most fully satisfied with our own strength, knowledge, and power. This is why pride is the greatest Christian sin. Not the kind of pride that unites us with others—*Black pride* or *Gay pride*—but the kind of pride that estranges us from God and our neighbors. If pride led Adam and Eve to eat the fruit of the tree of knowledge that they might become as gods, the fall humbled them into a state where they, and consequently we, regardless of our attainments, are made equal communicants of pain and death.

"We may know nothing of our destiny."

ECCLESIASTES 7:15

The lessons of the fall are lost on those who claim that special knowledge can protect us from suffering or give us power over our health and destiny. Modern spiritual teachings such as those contained in *A Course in Miracles* suggest that "Both sickness and health are in our control. . . . Problems exist only in the mind . . . The Holy Spirit will solve every problem." According to such teaching, if we align ourselves with truth or love, it will protect us, inoculating us against suffering, illness, and other afflictions that visit those who stand outside the circle of light.

Others contend that everything happens for a reason. For instance, if a young woman has cancer, it was meant to be, perhaps to test her faith and make her a better person or to punish her for something she did in this or some past life. Or maybe she got cancer because of her inabil-

ity to handle stress, her poor diet, or her failure to align
herself with the Holy. One way or another, by this way of
thinking we are held responsible for our own afflictions.

Several years ago a young woman I know suffered
an ectoptic pregnancy. Her fetus was developing outside
of the womb and had to be aborted. All she could think
was, "Why did this happen to me?" Several friends, fellow members of a group of New Age spiritual seekers,
had ready answers. "Nothing happens that we don't
choose for ourselves," one said. "Clearly you were ambiv-
alent about having a child. Sensing this, the baby balked
at coming into the world." To reconcile their friend to
her inevitable fate, others posited everything from bad
karma in a previous life to a new take on predestination
(women who can't bear children are not worthy of being
mothers).

This young woman had joined a New Age spiritual circle because she believed, as her friends did, that if we tap
the source of holiness all will be well with us. Today,
blessed with two lovely subsequent children and a deeper
appreciation for life's mystery, she views both her pain
and her joy in a different light. "I used to yearn to control
my environment and my future," she wrote me in a recent letter. "A tragic accident or loss like my lost pregnancy makes you give up that dream fast. The reward for
giving up that dream of control is that you are set free."

She learned something else as well. In this same letter,
she writes that, after she gave birth to her first child, "I
thought of all the women who were still aching as I had
been, and how they would continue to ache for months

or years, or maybe forever." Through her own experience of anguish, she had discovered a bridge to the hearts of others. This invested her newfound joy with a depth that otherwise it would have lacked. What her friends had not been able to offer her, she now can offer to others, a wisdom born of pain.

"Better one handful of repose than
two hands full of effort in chasing the wind."

ECCLESIASTES 4:6

People who claim that higher knowledge will
free us from suffering are fooling themselves. So too are
those who place their faith in a perfectly tuned and well-
fortified body. Don't get me wrong. It makes good sense
to take care of our bodies. But to do so to the point of obsession only invites another form of pride. I have a friend
who has given up alcohol, cigarettes, coffee, eggs, meat,
milk, and the sun. He eats oat bran for breakfast, takes
megadoses of vitamins C and E, rides his exercycle reli-
giously, and never uses his microwave oven.

Things are getting difficult for people who devote
their lives to postponing death. Almost every day something new is added to the list of death-abetting substances
and activities. The latest killer, believe it or not, is dreams.
According to a recent study, dreaming can be bad for our
health, because when we dream our heart rate jumps.

The more vivid the dream—vivid having nothing to do with good or bad—the more our heart rate jumps. And, according to medical experts, jumping heart rates can lead to heart attacks.

The good news is, unlike everything else we are supposed to avoid because it may lead to heart attacks, we can't do anything about our dreams. But even if we could, it wouldn't help. The hard truth is, we all die of something. Vegetarians die. Joggers die. Even people with low cholesterol die, many before their time. One can do everything imaginable to play the right numbers, to change the variables in our human equation, and still life won't check.

No one would dare blame a three-year-old who fell to her death for playing recklessly in a third-story window, even though the cause and effect in such a case is clear. Yet, oddly enough, many people who fall victim to mortal illness try desperately to figure out what they did wrong, so they can blame themselves. If we shoot ourselves in the head, death is our own fault. But even though smoking increases the likelihood of cancer, when a person dies at sixty-five of lung cancer, it's not only her fault, or the tobacco company's fault, or the fault of society for condoning smoking. When we die, however we may have lived, the ultimate culprit is not sin or squalor. The culprit is life. Life draws death in its glorious train.

The spiritual question suggested here addresses pride and its dangers. All who believe that they can fully control their destiny by proper attitude and correct behavior are playing God. The role is too big for us. A bit of sensible Stoicism is in order. Writing to his friend Lucilius, the Roman philosopher Seneca meditates on the vagaries of life and the folly of those who believe we can dictate our own destiny: "Sickness assails those leading the most sensible lives, tuberculosis those with the strongest constitutions, retribution the utterly guiltless, violence the most secluded. Misfortune has a way of choosing some unprecedented means or other of impressing its power on those who might be said to have forgotten it."

The temptation to assume that if we live right, we will somehow outwit illness and death is no less blasphemous than to consider fleshly living as nothing but a grim and dangerous precursor to angelic purity.

Obviously it's healthful to cut back on foods that may not be good for us. I haven't had a cheeseburger in months (well, maybe one or two!), and my life is not appreciably diminished. If we follow doctor's orders, change our diet, and treat our bodies like temples, we will probably feel better and may live a little longer. But we will end up just as dead as our least prudent neighbor. He may even outlive us.

Adolf Hitler was into purity in a big way. He neither smoked nor drank, discouraged the eating of red meat, developed sparkling water at Dachau, and established a national fitness program. Then he sought to "purify" the national gene pool by exterminating six million Jews. I reject the glib term "health Nazis" for today's fitness zealots. But cleansing our bodies has little to do with loving our neighbor as ourselves. Instead it may lead to a judgmental, highly moralistic attitude toward our neighbor. However long we live, life is too short for that.

The question remains, what are we living long *for*? For ourselves? To live a hundred years? We live longer today than our ancestors did, especially our ancient ancestors. Alexander the Great had entered what people then considered middle age when he died at thirty-three. So had Jesus. At the turn of the last century, in this very country, the average life span was less than fifty years. What was our great-grandparents' goal in life? Was it to outlive their ancestors, or to leave something for future generations that would make us proud of them?

These are not idle thoughts. I've just turned forty-seven. When Martin Luther King, Jr., was my age he had been dead nine years. Robert Kennedy, four. Anne Frank, thirty-one. Each lived in such a way that life proved worth dying for.

"Better two than one by himself."

I learned this lesson first from Dalton Denton. Dalton was my closest friend at Stanford. During the middle of our sophomore year he died of pneumonia while on a skiing vacation at Vail, Colorado. He had been out on the slopes just the day before. That morning he felt a little tired and somewhat congested, so he stayed in the cabin while his friends skied. When they returned home later in the afternoon, Dalton was dead.

Dalton was a blithe spirit, serious about life but not at all somber. He was tremendous fun to be with, and we spent almost all our free time together. He introduced me to Scotch and Beethoven, two habits he had picked up at Exeter. I suppose that he was the closest thing to a sophisticate I had ever encountered. We were dorm-mates in our freshman year. Together we pursued—he successfully, I not—two striking girls, both actresses, who

25

were themselves best friends. More than once after an all-night conversation, Dalton and I saw in the dawn.

At the beginning of our sophomore year, Dalton, five other friends of ours, and I moved into the Theta Xi fraternity house. The previous spring we had rushed as a group. The rules we set up for ourselves were clearly stated from the outset. If any one of us was not acceptable, none of us would accept the fraternity's bid. To insure the success of this enterprise we chose the weakest fraternity on campus.

I scorned the fraternity system almost as much as other people in the system scorned Theta Xi. The plan that my friends and I concocted was simple. We would move in and quickly take over the house. The price was right, and being located on campus, it would serve as a convenient commune. The seven of us did constitute a majority of the fall pledge class that year at Theta Xi. But taking over was not as simple a matter as I imagined it would be.

One night, after a particularly raucous party, we pledges were awakened from our beds and lined up downstairs in our underwear. I had not even considered the possibility: we were about to be hazed. The first act of obedience that was required of us was the first of many I refused to perform. It was three o'clock in the morning, and I was not about to put a piece of liver down my shorts. As I look back on it, the two most surprising things about the following twenty-four hours were, first, that no one forced me to do anything, and second, that all of my friends were perfectly happy to go along with whatever games they were told to play.

At the end of what was surely the mildest hell week in fraternity history, my friends and I were taught the secret handshake and inducted into the brotherhood. Two weeks later, having found an apartment underneath a house nestled in the foothills above Stanford, I left Theta Xi. Dalton was hurt and angry. He accused me of petulance and unwarranted pride. I accused him of succumbing to a foolish, childish set of rules and rites. For almost two months we did not speak to one another. During this same period I almost left Stanford. I went home to Idaho during Thanksgiving break. My courses were not going well, and I compounded the problem by staying away for three weeks. My father prevailed upon me to return to school at least to finish the year. I dropped one course and salvaged the three others. Nevertheless, I remained alone, distant from my friends and wholly without bearings.

A week before Dalton died, he surprised me one morning by arriving at my burrow in the woods, and we went on a long drive together. All day long, we drove back and forth along the highway between Stanford and the sea. We talked about friendship, meaning, and death.

This meeting of hearts and minds was surely less profound than memory suggests. As often with true friendship, we passed a good part of that time, I am sure, simply enjoying one another's company: exchanging insults with the immunity that love bestows, delighting in word games and frivolous repartee, talking a private language that only the two of us could fully understand.

Yet, there were serious moments. These were the moments I remember. I told Dalton that I did not expect to live past the age of twenty-five. This was part of a romantic, melodramatic attempt to feel life deeply, at a time when I was struggling to feel anything at all. Dalton was sympathetic but unimpressed. It was enough, he told me, to live and love as best we could.

What a blessing that day was. It resulted in a total reconciliation. And his love that day was not the final gift Dalton gave to me. That gift came in self-renewing and ever-increasing installments after he died. It is the gift of memory. I had lost someone I loved. Each time I remember him, our last day together, the twinkle in his eye, I awaken again to how fragile life is and how precious.

Both before he died and as a consequence of his death, Dalton also taught me how much courage it takes to love. Whenever we give our hearts in love, the burden of our vulnerability grows. We risk being rebuffed or embarrassed or inadequate. Beyond these things, we risk the enormous pain of loss. When those we love die, a part of us dies with them. When those we love are sick, in body or spirit, we too feel the pain.

All of this is worth it. Especially the pain. If we insulate our hearts from suffering, we shall only subdue the very thing that makes life worth living. We cannot protect ourselves from loss. We can only protect ourselves from the death of love. And without love, there is no meaning. Without love, we are left only with the aching hollow of regret, that haunting emptiness where love might have been.

"Naked from her mother's womb she came,
as naked as she came she will depart again."

ECCLESIASTES 5:14

The encounter of love and death is always wrenching, but never more so than for a parent who loses a child.

When Cassie came into the world, three generations rejoiced. First, her parents. With a new appreciation for the miracle of life, they had cause for great thanksgiving. Her grandparents, too, had special reason to celebrate. On one side she was the first grandchild; on the other, the first girl after four boys. As for her great-grandmother, she laughed and said, "Clearly, I haven't lived too long."

Cassie was three months old before her loved ones suspected that something was terribly wrong. She ate well and cried her little heart out and looked as beautiful as a baby can look, which is very beautiful indeed. But she didn't respond to bright colors or loud noises and had trouble raising her head. After weeks of inconclusive test-

29

ing, Cassie's parents had their worst fears confirmed. She had been born with a rare congenital disease. Special medications might help, but some of these, such as steroids, could be given only in limited doses, to protect her kidneys from secondary complications. Little hope was offered.

Cassie's father was a realist. "How long does she have?" he asked. Having seen such tragedies unfold before, I knew he might have posed this question differently. "How long do we have, and what are the odds on our making it?"

"Five, ten years. One never knows," the doctor replied. The watch began.

So what would you say to this young couple, hoping against hope, facing the diminishing life and almost certain early death of their baby daughter? Perhaps only this. Be gentle with one another. Forgive the world. And remember, we tend to rise in response to tragedy. Whatever hand we may be dealt, perhaps because it's our own hand, not someone else's, we often play it better than another could imagine doing in our stead.

And what if we don't? If we fold under the pressure, what then?

Well, that's all right too. If we can't forgive the world for our pain and ourselves for our failure to endure it, a forgiving world will embrace us. We can lean on its strong shoulders and cry our hearts out.

Cassie's disease would not go away, no matter how hard her parents prayed or her doctors tried. When she was

four years old, she couldn't talk, but she could walk a little, respond readily to others, and take real delight in life.

Always the first to see McDonald's Golden Arches
from miles away down the highway, she knew as well as
any four-year-old how to cajole her parents into stopping. They, in turn, lived for the slightest breakthrough
in her precious development. But that's not all they lived
for. They also lived for one another and for their neighbors. Even when their daughter's health continued to de-
teriorate. Even when, after suffering a series of setbacks,
she became completely disabled and finally housebound,
they struggled and they thrived.

Thrived is probably too strong a word. But that's what
the world saw. Two lovely people, outgoing, active in their
church, attentive to their friends, successful in their
work.

Cassie finally died. Life was too much for her little
body to sustain.

"It's interesting," this sweet little girl's mother said to
me. "Sometimes I get the feeling that other people have
a harder time dealing with it than we do. It's so real to us.
We know what we've lost. But other people can't face it.
They can't talk about it. They're frightened."

"They're frightened of us too," her husband added,
"as if we had some kind of disease that they might catch
if they got too close." Or say the wrong thing, I thought
sheepishly to myself.

"We're doing pretty well," he continued. "My wife's
right about that. But we could sure use some help and not

just from the therapist we're going to. On any given day, one of us may need to work on the past, focus on the present, or make future plans. Yet with the whole world, our family and friends, tiptoeing around us, we are left almost wholly dependent upon one another."

"It's funny," she added. "Though most people can't seem to handle talking about Cassie's death, are awkward around us and even shy away sometimes, when we are together with them, laughing or chatting about some silly thing, I get this odd feeling that we're being judged, as if our behavior was somehow inappropriate."

We went on talking about the conspiracy of silence involving death, about how the most natural thing in the world has been turned into a monster that people are frightened even to name, about Cassie, about their decision to try to have another child.

"I know one thing," her mother added in a bright, clear voice. "Now, when someone I know loses a loved one, I'll be there with a casserole and all the time in the world."

"No one can say that eyes have not had enough of seeing, ears their fill of hearing."

ECCLESIASTES 1:8

The world's great religions offer differing interpretations of suffering, but all acknowledge that it lies at the very heart of human experience.

In the Buddhist scriptures, there is a parable about a woman whose child died. In her disbelief and anguish, she accosted a local guru, begging him to intercede and return her child to life. He agrees. "All you have to do," he says to the distraught woman, "is bring me a grain of rice from a household that has escaped the curse of grief." With great hope, she goes through her village, door by door, and then through the neighboring village, only to hear story upon story of suffering and loss. Finally she returns to the guru, no less in pain, but far wiser, more compassionate, and willing to accept her human lot.

Prince Siddhārtha Gautama, the man who became the Buddha, was born into royalty. His father was king of a tiny state in northeastern India. Many legends grew up surrounding Siddhārtha's birth. In one his mother, Maya, was visited in a dream by a white elephant, the Indian equivalent of the Holy Spirit, who touched her side and quickened her womb. Upon hearing this, her husband called on his wisest counselors, seeking their interpretation of her dream. They prophesied the birth of a remarkable child, one destined to be either a world ruler, or, should he choose the path of religion, a universal savior.

Like most fathers, the king hoped that his son would amount to something when he grew up. Accordingly, he sought a way to guarantee that the boy would choose politics over religion. The wise men told him that there was only one way to ensure this. He must shield Siddhārtha from all acquaintance with old age, sickness, and death.

And so Prince Siddhārtha lived his youth in ignorance of the world's ills. Not only were old age, sickness, and death veiled from his sight, but every imaginable sensual delight was lavished on him so that he would never be tempted to explore outside his bubble world. His father gave him three palaces, one for each season of the Indian year, and distracted him with dancing girls, jugglers, storytellers, and gaming companions. Whenever Siddhārtha desired to venture into the outside world, his wish was granted, as were all his wishes, but with this one condition. The way was carefully plotted, his route swept clean of all reminders of mortality, and the streets festooned with banners and populated with playing children and dancing youths.

One day, as usual, Siddhārtha and his charioteer drove out into the world in his gilded chariot. But when they reached the country roads, his eye caught sight of something wildly at variance with anything he had ever seen before: a bent old man with a wizened face, hobbling along with a cane in his hand.

"What sort of man is this, if indeed it is a man?" Siddhārtha asked his driver.

Not knowing how to evade the truth, his companion replied, "This is a man in old age. Once he was a babe, then a youth, and then a man in full strength and beauty. But now his strength and beauty are gone. He is withered and wasted. It is the way of all flesh."

The next day, the specter of a sick person, prostrate, groaning, and emaciated, appeared along their route. When Siddhārtha asked, "What manner of person is this?" his charioteer could only reply that each of us is prey to sickness in this life.

Finally and inevitably, despite his father's precautions, the young prince and his driver encountered a funeral procession. The attendants following a corpse on a bier were weeping, tearing their clothing, and beating their breasts. Again, in response to Siddhārtha's bewilderment, his companion explained, "It is death. He has been taken from those he loves, and from his home. His life is ended." The prince asked, "Are there other dead people?" To which the charioteer replied, "All who are born must die. There is no way of escape."

Such was the nature of Siddhārtha's first awakening. Having come face to face with his mortality and all the suffering and illness that it entailed, he found his life—despite all its pleasures—hollow at the core, empty of any consciousness of ultimate things. And so he began his pilgrimage.

The Buddha's journey led him to seek a way beyond suffering, a truth that would leave him invulnerable to life's certain pains. The Christian path is different. Through the passion of Christ, the gospels teach that redemption entails sacrifice. Vulnerability is the keystone of Jesus's gospel. But both scriptures have this in common: The beginning of enlightenment comes through an encounter with suffering and death.

In perhaps his most famous sermon, the Buddha painted human life as a soul on fire. Everything visible is in flames. Our lives run the gamut from pleasure to pain, from lust and fascination to sorrow, grief, and despair. The passions we experience are kindled by desire. "The ear is in flames, the tongue is in flames; the body is in flames; the mind is in flames." He believed that, to put out the fire, we must quench desire. "Free from desire" we are delivered. "Rebirth is at an end, perfected is holiness, duty done; there is no more returning to this world."

In Western thought the closest philosophy to Buddhism is the cosmic pessimism of Stoicism, a Greek school of philosophy that flourished around the time of Jesus. Taking as their model the death of Socrates, the Stoics fashioned a stark response to life's exigencies. "We must get rid of this craving for life," wrote the Roman philosopher Seneca, "and learn that it makes no difference when your suffering comes, because at some time you are bound to suffer." As a philosophical attitude, the Stoics proposed apathy, a word that now carries the negative connotation of not caring but then suggested freedom from the vulnerability inherent in feeling. Detachment was their antidote to desire and the inevitable disappointments that would follow all attempts to love and prosper. Accomplished Stoics were nothing if not courageous in the face of tragedy and loss. They also knew that if we care too much about anything beyond our control, we leave ourselves open to the whims of fate, even at our moment of greatest happiness or triumph.

In contrast to their contemporaries the Epicureans (not hedonists like their modern namesakes, but devotees of moderation), the Stoics played on a larger stage. They embraced duty, not pleasure, as the goal of life, and this duty was owed to God. Good Stoics didn't avoid risk or conflict simply because they might fail or be wounded. They sought to free themselves from unproductive concern about the inevitable reversals of human fortune.

Despite the underlying basis of pessimism that informs Buddhism and Stoicism, both combine a realistic assessment of suffering with a social conscience, the former driven by compassion, the latter by duty. Each faith is unintentionally life-affirming, for life is enhanced by the efforts of their most noble adherents.

Similar dark currents flow through Christianity, even if the results are not always this ennobling. I think of St. Hillary. Distressed that his daughter was being sought in marriage by a nobleman, and committed to extricating her from the snare of earthly pleasures, Hillary begged her to reject her suitor's proposal. When she balked, he countered by praying for her death. Months later, when she actually did die, he rejoiced unceasingly.

This story has an even grimmer codicil. Hillary informed his wife that, through prayer, he had delivered their daughter from the arms of lust and mammon into the arms of God. She begged him to release her as well, and so the two of them prayed together day and night for her deliverance. According to legend, God obliged.

At its most severe, which we witness here, the obsession with transcending human feeling is life-denying. Take away the speculative prospect of an afterlife, and one is left with the radical pessimism of someone like the nihilist philosopher Schopenhauer, who, in his book *The Vanity of Existence*, wrote that "human life must be some kind of mistake." Even wrapped in the more noble cloak of Buddhism and Stoicism, the proposed deprivation of feeling and passion (as a means to liberate us from the inevitable suffering that accompanies human attachment) represents a negative life force. Yet, life denial remains a completely plausible response to life's pain, one far from restricted to the annals of religious asceticism or human pathology.

The Greek historian Herodotus tells the story of the Trausi tribe in Africa. "When a child is born to them, all its kindred sit round about it in a circle and weep for the woes it will have to undergo now that it is come into the world, making mention of every ill that falls to the lot of humankind; when, on the other hand, a man has died, they bury him with laughter and rejoicings, and say that now he is free from a host of sufferings, and enjoys the completest happiness." In this same spirit, the Preacher in Ecclesiastes writes, "So, rather than the living who still have lives to live, I salute the dead who have already met death; happier than both of these is he who is yet unborn."

However perverse this may seem, it does add a patina of realism to the picture of life we too often try to paint for ourselves. As with the pastel icon of Jesus that hung over my bed when I was a child—pink-faced, cloaked in baby blue, and sweet with a halo—even when it comes to our saviors we tend to wish away the darkness. Then, when darkness falls, we are not prepared. The Trausi and their soulmates may rob from life its joy, but at least they acknowledge the inevitability of pain.

I don't accept this nihilistic, or nirvanic—both words suggest nothingness—resolution of our human quest for enlightenment and salvation. But the truth it points to cannot be gainsaid. Life is painful, and passion or desire, when thwarted, can be agonizing. The message of Genesis and the story of the Buddha's enlightenment are in this respect one.

Once we understand this truth, how do we respond? Siddhārtha's pilgrimage led him first to self-abnegation. He deprived himself of every possible stimulus, including food. Meditating for hours, sometimes days at a time, he attempted to cleanse his body and mind of all desire.

A similar quest for complete freedom from every attachment bedeviled the early Christian Desert Fathers. To escape, or deny, all human passions, which they believed separated them from a pure love of God, they retreated to the desert and devoted their lives to prayer and self-discipline. There was only one remaining problem. Sometimes, the harder they tried not to think about sex and food, the more powerful these images became. When this happened, judging from the extant sayings of certain Desert Fathers, more than a few of them ended up hating themselves all the more for their weakness, assuming that human nature could be contraverted by an act of will. The wisest of the Desert Fathers, recognizing this as a form of pride, preached a gentler gospel, accepting of imperfection. But many held hard to purity, only to find themselves broken on the rocks of their own inevitable need.

Siddhārtha, now the Buddha Gautama, grew out of this phase. His enlightenment followed on the recognition that the more preoccupied we are with our demons, the stronger they grow. Under the Bodhi tree he realized that abstinence weakens the soul by making it more vulnerable. The true way cannot be gained, he later preached, "by one who has lost his strength."

Gautama's return to the world he sought ultimately to escape represented an incomplete conversion. Women, most poignantly his wife, continued to threaten his peace of mind and led him, initially, to exclude them from his circle of followers. But he did begin to eat again, took his body a little less seriously, and finally, responding to his wife's noble importunity, even accepted women, with some restrictions, onto the training grounds for Nirvana.

Over time, the Buddhists developed two schools. One followed the narrow road, holding to the extinction of desire as a direct ticket to Nirvana, the end of suffering. The other, Mahayana Buddhism, proposed a different ideal, the Bodhisattva, one who would continue to return through one incarnation after another until no other creature remained unenlightened. Bodhisattvas chose to reject the ultimate comforts of Nirvana until all suffering, not only their own, was expunged from human experience. This school of Buddhism holds that none of us lives unto ourselves alone. We share one another's suffering and pain. So long as others suffer, we too must suffer with and for them.

In contrast to the Buddhist (and Stoic) ideal of detachment or dispassion, the ancient Hebrews honored suffering, viewing it as a sign of deeply felt experience, a symbol of their passion. I encountered an intimate expression of this on a recent visit to Israel.

The Israel Museum in Jerusalem contains a collection of tiny ceramic cups. These were sacramental vessels. People cried into them.

Your mother has just died. Someone you love has cancer. Your spouse has left you. You are struggling at work. More likely, you have simply broken down. You burst into tears. So you pick up your tear cup, put it under your eye, and weep into it. When you are finished weeping, you cap it and put it away again. It is a way to save your tears.

Why save them? Because they are precious. It doesn't matter why you cried, your tears are still precious, for they show that you care. A full cup of tears is proof that you have felt deeply, suffered, and survived. Their value is ratified by this simple parable from Jewish lore. When his student complained that he was suffering and so deeply confused that he could no longer pray and study, Rebbe Mendl of Kotzk asked him, "What if God prefers your tears to your studying?"

If we knew better, we would cry far more often than we do. Life is difficult. Some people pretend that it is not, that we should be able to breeze through. Yet hardly a week passes in which most of us don't have something worth crying about.

Men seem to have a particularly hard time with this. We are taught not to cry. Tough it out. Don't let your feelings show, lest you be perceived as weak and soft. Yet, at times of loss, an acknowledgment of weakness and softness suggests a tender heart. If there is a single person who can't find something worth crying about, I would not like to meet him.

Many of us men have a hard time crying because we are afraid of our feelings. Every time we express ourselves emotionally, we lose some control. As the self-protected, fully armored husband in Wallace Stegner's novel *The Spectator Bird*, says to his wife, "If we could peel off the callus, and wanted to, there we would be, untouched by time, unwithered, vulnerable, afflicted and volatile and blind to consequence, a set of twitches as beyond control as an adolescent's erections." Yet, for those of us who become proficient at maintaining control, the results can be even more disastrous. We take our feelings and strangle them. Then we are nothing but closed, tight, frightened little people, pretending that we have grown up and hoping that no one will notice how deeply we really do care. At first it is an act, a hard act, but over time, as we get better at it, it may become less difficult, perhaps because we really do not care any longer. If we fail to practice caring, hurting, and crying, over time we may forget how.

On the surface, this has advantages. A callused heart remains invulnerable. The best way to protect ourselves from being wounded is to avoid love, or to love only in little ways so that when we are hurt we will only hurt in little ways. That was not the fashion among the ancient Hebrews. They were not afraid to cry. Their tears were sacraments of love, which flowed from a deep spring. The fuller one's tear cup, the more a person was esteemed. Great-hearted people, it seems, cried far more readily than small-hearted people. Life touched them more deeply, not only the pain of it but also the joy. They wept into their cups of tears until they could truly say, "My cup runneth over."

"Better the end of a matter than its beginning,
better patience than pride."

ECCLESIASTES 7:8–9

If suffering may be expressed nobly, it can also drown a struggling soul. This is one reason that suffering cannot be considered good in itself. Yet the same crisis that destroys one life can, in another, usher in transformation. In the world of substance abusers, one well-known form of this is referred to as "hitting bottom."

Late one evening, I received an emergency call from the hospital. A member of my congregation was in intensive care. They told me he wouldn't make it through the night. I rushed over and found him in an alcoholic coma. This was no surprise. The man had been drinking himself to death for years.

I worked up my courage (those who claim that intensive care units don't inspire fear are probably lying), entered the sixteen-bed unit, and found him unconscious in stall number nine. Looking down at him, emaciated, attached to a respirator, I muttered a prayer and said good-bye.

So much for appearances. Two days later, he emerged from the coma. Not that winning back his life seemed all that great a prize. Sure, he had beaten death, but for what? His world was a shambles: a broken marriage (with plenty of blame to go around), desperate children, and angry creditors. Just the sort of situation that might drive a man to drink. But he didn't drink. Instead he swallowed his pride, declared bankruptcy, filed for divorce, became a single parent, got his kids in a support group, and began attending Alcoholic Anonymous meetings. Piece by piece, he began putting his life back together.

Once a respected writer, when this man set out looking for work he found himself blackballed for having missed so many deadlines. He settled for a job behind the counter of a deli. I asked him about this. "I like it," he said. "After all, I am alive, and it pays the bills." He worked there for a year. Following the counsel of Alcoholics Anonymous, he chose not to risk his recovery by making any major changes during his first year sober.

His children continue healing from the wounds inflicted by their father's disease. But with the help of Al-Anon, both are doing better than I ever thought they would. I celebrated his daughter's wedding this past spring, twelve years after her father's brush with death. For a time, he lived in Los Angeles, writing for a successful TV series. He now is remarried and has retired to Maine. He speaks easily, and with hard-won humility, about a Higher Power. Almost every Easter, he sends me a letter. Life is difficult. He is fine. Easter is his favorite holiday.

"A generation goes, a generation comes."

ECCLESIASTES 1:4

Easter is a story of love and death. Jesus's disciples expected him to live and save them. But Jesus did not live and save them. He died and saved them, which is all the more powerful, however you choose to interpret it. Even after death, Jesus lived on in his disciples' hearts. Everything that mattered about him was theirs now. The way he cast out fear with faith. His love of God and neighbor. His astonishing humility. His disdain for pretense and cant. His courage and his passion. Each was more present than ever before because Jesus now lived *within* them, not simply *among* them.

For us too, death is love's measure. Not only is our grief when someone dies testimony to our love, but when we ourselves die, the love we have given to others is the one thing death can't kill. Only our unspent love dies when we die, love unspent because of fear. It is fear that locks love in the prison of our hearts, there to be buried with us.

Because we and our loved ones manage to devise so many ways for fear to bind our hearts—fear of intimacy, disappointment, embarrassment, confrontation—we often hurt one another without really meaning to. We hurt one another by learning, over the practice of a lifetime, how to protect ourselves from pain. Add to this all the mistakes we make and all the mistakes others make, and forgiveness becomes essential. Only a heart capable of accepting and bestowing forgiveness is open to give and receive the saving power of love. This is the essence of Jesus' gospel. We all are children of God. We all are sinners. We can be forgiven, if we will refrain from harsh judgment. Love casts out fear. God is love. And love never dies.

Think about your parents—at least the great majority of parents, parents who love their children. So much of what they likely felt or feel toward you, you will never know. But you may feel it in turn, toward children of your own, surmising from this what your parents may have felt. Their amazement at your birth. The way they cradled you, helpless, wholly dependent, in their arms. Their unconditional love, however imperfectly expressed. How they sacrificed for you. You really never knew. You couldn't know. How they suffered when you burned with fever as a baby. How much your pains in growing hurt them. How they wished they might suffer for you, protect you, make you safe from others and yourself, even from them, from all the inherited and ac-

49

quired quirks and flaws they brought to hearth and table. But they couldn't. And they probably knew they couldn't. They knew that nothing in their power, no amount of caring, even were they to do the impossible and get everything right, could protect you finally, either from life or from death. Another thing is true of them, at least for most of them. They knew or know that you will never fully realize how deeply they loved you, not only because of their own failures as parents or people, but also because children, even grown children, cannot know these things, not really. Yet, when your parents die, if they let you and you let them, their love will live on in your heart.

Every Easter is the same, only the company changes. Children go on to become parents. Parents, grandparents. We are in large measure heedless, both of the passing of time and of the diseases or accidents hidden from our sight yet present in prospect in time's frame. In a haunting poem, "Easter Sunday, 1955," Elizabeth Spires looks at an old photograph.

> . . . No one has died yet.
> No vows have been broken. No words spoken
> that can never be taken back, never forgotten.
> I have a basket of eggs my mother and I dyed yesterday.
> I ask my grandmother to choose one, just one,
> and she takes me up—O hold me close!—
> her cancer not yet diagnosed. I bury my face
> in soft flesh, the soft folds of her Easter dress,
> breathing her in, wanting to stay forever where I am.

But we can't stay forever where we are. We don't even know where we are, until after we have been there, until we look back to see what happened, ten, twenty, thirty Easters later.

> *. . . Now my daughter steps*
> *into the light, her basket of eggs bright, so bright.*
> One, choose one, *I hear her say, her face upturned*
> *to mine, innocent of outcome. Beautiful child,*
> *how thoughtlessly we enter the world!*
> *How free we are, how bound, put here in love's name*
> *—death's, too—to be happy if we can.*

"Where were we?" we ask ourselves. "What have we become? Will anything we do or feel today remain?"

Only love remains, only the love we give away.

"A time to plant;
a time to uproot what is planted."

Elisabeth Kübler-Ross once wrote that, "Should you shield the canyons from the windstorms, you would never see the beauty of their carvings."

Two winters ago, a long-standing member of All Souls took her own life. She suffered from inoperable liver cancer. When presented with her alternatives, she decided first, not to try to prolong her life with drugs, and then, to choose her own time to leave.

I first met her—an elegant, confident woman—when her husband was stricken by cancer twelve years before. He wished to die at home. The doctors were not sure that this was prudent. This particular couple didn't give a fig for prudence. I remember so vividly their lying on the bed together, going through old picture albums, watching the U.S. Open on television. He faded quickly, then he died. Both of them were at peace.

This same woman went on to help organize the New York chapter of the Hemlock Society. Its meetings are held at our church. This makes me a little uncomfortable, but she didn't make me uncomfortable. Her major issue was the cost to society of futile health care for the mortally ill. When she told me she was dying and of her plans —two wonderful trips, one to Wyoming, the other to Alaska—but also of her determination to choose the moment she would die, I could only admire her. She might have lived a few weeks longer, but she died well.

I had a long talk with her the day she died. I asked her if she was frightened.

"A little," she replied.

"It's such a mystery," I said. "Who knows what happens after we die."

"I do," she answered. "I'm going to be part of the stars." Whether literally or metaphorically doesn't really matter. She is now part of the stars.

Three months before she died, this courageous woman wrote a poem which she gave to me. It closes with the words:

These days I take nothing for granted.
Neither memories, nor the good smell of morning toast.
Still nimble, my body follows all orders,
And all five senses are acute.

When did you last pause to offer thanks that your senses were acute?

PART II

Original Guilt:
Lifelines to Self-Acceptance
& Forgiveness

"I find that God made human beings simple;
their complex problems are of their own devising."

ECCLESIASTES 7:30

The lifelines that support us are not complicated in and of themselves. Each has two ends, the one we hold and the one that connects us to others. Yet human nature is such that we often manage to get our lifelines crossed. Sometimes we demand more of ourselves and others than either we or they are able to deliver. Harsh judgments, both inner criticism and criticism directed at our neighbors, estrange us from our source of connection. Jealousy, anger, bitterness, disappointment, fear of intimacy, failure—all the pains that accompany any human relationship—can cut us off from sources of comfort and strength. At the signing of the Declaration of Independence, Benjamin Franklin said to John Hancock, "We must indeed all hang together, or, most assuredly, we shall all hang separately." This is as true of personal relationships as it is of nation states.

To secure both ends of our lifelines, two things are necessary: self-acceptance and forgiveness. It is possible to establish sustaining human bonds, but to do so with any degree of security we must first accept our human foibles and forgive others theirs. Since everyone fails, suffers, grieves, and dies, this should be simple. But our nature is to make simple things complicated. In Christian theology, the name for this is "original sin." One might think of it also as "original guilt." Guilt, both perceived and actual, is endemic to human experience. Until we can accept this of ourselves and forgive others for it, no lifeline exists that will connect our hearts.

This goes for us and our parents, children, spouses, friends, coworkers, neighbors, even enemies. We share more than divides us, but some of the things we hold in common conspire to separate us from one another. To secure lifelines that will hold when darkness falls and hope wanes, we must reckon with our all-too-human potential to subvert ourselves and one another.

"There is no virtuous person on earth who,
doing good, is ever free of sin."

ECCLESIASTES 7:20

I begin my observations on the nature of human nature with an illusively simple question. Why do we shake hands when we greet? Until I discovered the genesis of the handshake, I assumed it had to do with our storied friendliness and informality. I was wrong. The handshake started in Europe in the early Middle Ages. Men shook hands when they met; women did not. The reason men shook hands is that they were checking one another for concealed weapons.

And how about the clinking of glasses that follows a toast? How did that delightful custom come about? It happened this way. After checking for concealed weapons, a party of men would gather around a table for food and drink. They clinked glasses in order to pour some of their wine into one another's cups. They were protecting themselves from being poisoned.

Two of the most convivial of customs arose therefore from suspicion. A stranger, even a host or a guest, was presumed guilty until proven innocent. I welcome you into my home, but only after assuring myself that you are not armed. When I then offer you wine, you in turn make certain that I've done nothing to doctor it. All of this is performed with hearty protestations of affability. "Hail and welcome, my dear friend!" And then, in gracious answer, "Cheers. To your health." What they are really saying is, "I don't trust you, my friend." And then, in answer, "Cheers. Have some of mine. If it's poison, you're dead." Suspicion disguised as friendliness turns out to be a primary source for the development of civility.

Theologians have argued over the question of human nature for centuries. Are we born good or are we sinners? Should we love our neighbors, check them for weapons, or both? Liberal theologians tend to paint a rosy picture of human nature: good out of the blocks and then tainted by society. More orthodox students view us as intrinsically flawed but capable of redemption. I am strangely amenable to both positions. From my observation, we are basically good yet intrinsically flawed; society taints us but also tempers us, and we are capable of redemption. In fact, our acknowledging a sense of guilt may be proof of our basic goodness. Given a positive rather than negative spin, it may also facilitate redemption.

We are all guilty. Most of the crimes we commit are not horrid, simply human—crimes punishable only by conscience. Our consciences sometimes fall asleep or are lulled or drugged, and we do bad things we don't notice, at least for the time being. We also manage to blame others for our own actions or rationalize our behavior through some convenient trick of mind. But more often we convict ourselves in the tribunal of conscience. Every day we find reasons to judge and then punish ourselves for what we do or fail to do. Some of this punishment is justified. Much is not. In either case, we spend a fair portion of our conscious lives on the lam, running from ourselves and others and hoping not to get caught.

But we are not only guilty; we are also innocent. This matter of innocence complicates things, because death, grief, and illness, even prejudice and ignorance, have far less to do with our behavior than with our humanity.

I think of my parishioners. How often they come to me upset with themselves for not getting life right. Having seen or read so many of the advertisements for enlightenment, having tried one recipe after another for happiness, they still feel weak, inadequate, even incompetent for not being "better" or "wiser" than they are. If sick, they often seek to blame themselves. If broken by a string of catastrophes, they wonder why they are not stronger, or why these things happened to them. If depressed, they search for answers, fail to find them, and despair. They measure their lives against unachievable standards. They compare themselves to others, whose masks they cannot see through, and come up wanting. At other times, when afflicted, they concentrate all their energies on trying to identify a culprit. Since life should not be like this, when things go wrong, even things that can't be helped, they reason that it must be either their own fault or someone else's.

I recognize these symptoms of guilt and judgment because I suffer from them too. When we seek what cannot be secured, strive to explain what cannot be fathomed, hold what is not ours to keep, be who we cannot become, we are invariably disappointed with ourselves and with others. Conversely, when we lapse into fatalism concerning things within our human power to shape or change, we are equally diminished. Of all the little crimes we commit against ourselves and others these are the most tragic, for they poison the wellspring of our life together. When we judge ourselves according to our failures to obtain the unobtainable, or remain locked in prisons with the key to freedom hidden in our pocket, parole for all lesser sins is fleeting and pardon impossible.

Any spiritual discipline worth the name is powered in part by justifiable guilt over the way we treat others. Even as we can, if often with great difficulty and over a long period of time, reform our fleshly behavior, a penitent spirit can spur the conscience beyond self-condemnation to corrective action in matters of the heart. In this sense, when we repent we are eligible for parole. Yet, when it comes to our life sentences (which we receive at birth), parole is not sufficient, at least not for most of us. What we need, therefore, and in the depth of our beings desire, is pardon. Not so much pardon for our crimes, but in a much larger sense pardon—"to pass over without punishment or blame"—for our humanity.

Sorting out what we can and cannot shape and control is one measure of the heart's wisdom. This practical philosophy finds its clearest expression in the serenity prayer, written by Reinhold Niebuhr and adapted as follows by twelve-step groups as the cornerstone of their teaching.

God grant us the serenity to accept the things
*   we cannot change,*
Courage to change the things we can,
And wisdom to know the difference.

When this prayer is answered, not only for those struggling with addiction, but for any of us as we struggle with the living and dying of our days, the serenity, courage, and wisdom we experience offer both parole and pardon. It has happened in my own life, and for more than twenty years as a pastor and counselor I have witnessed its power in the lives of many others. Openness to what we can change combined with an acceptance of all we cannot is the surest formula I know for the good life.

The good life would be an impossible dream were it not for our potential, even essential, goodness. This goodness is not displaced by our sense of guilt. On the contrary. Our conscience, even a guilty conscience, even sometimes an unnecessarily guilty conscience, is the emblem of goodness in our heart.

"Pay no attention to telltales;
you may hear that your servant has reviled you; your own
heart knows how often you have reviled others."

ECCLESIASTES 7:22

Who decides our guilt or innocence?

Think about it this way. Each of our lives is a trial by jury. By what we say and do, we supply evidence reflecting on our character, motives, and accomplishments to a jury of our peers. Some of this evidence is flattering, some really quite damning. All of it is open to interpretation.

Every day judgments are made about us on partial evidence by our loved ones, friends, colleagues, acquaintances, or even absolute strangers. The validity of these judgments is further compromised by the way in which the evidence is presented and affected by the context in which it and we are made known. We get accused of things we have not done. We also get away with things that no one notices. Throughout our life's trial, new evidence may alter others' judgments about us, or be dismissed for not fitting into preconceived notions they have developed over time.

In our lives, the jury is never out. Its judgments are sequential, sometimes spontaneous, often capricious. Sometimes we participate in our own defense, sometimes we leave our case to others. And, simultaneously, we ourselves sit on a thousand other juries, weighing evidence, making judgments, often as severe toward others as they can be toward us.

If the American justice system is flawed, our personal spins on justice are downright subversive. Hearsay (secondhand reports based on rumor) rarely gets thrown out. Trivial evidence often becomes primary. And since each of us is judge, jury, witness, and defendant in our life trials, there is no such thing as an objective opinion.

Ultimately our conscience is the only judgment that matters. Not that what the jury thinks doesn't matter; we can't help caring about what people think of us, how they behave toward us, what they say about us. But remember, for every instance that someone judges us falsely, in a way unflattering or hurtful to us, the odds are that someone else is judging us falsely in a flattering way, giving us credit where credit is not due.

I was falsely accused of lying the other day. It was something small, but it bothered me greatly. I mentioned this to my eldest son. "Why are you so upset about this, Dad?" he asked. "It's no big deal."

"What about you?" I continued. "When someone accuses you of something you did not do, how do you feel?"

"Well, for one thing," he said. "There's usually at least some truth on both sides."

I didn't want to hear this. On this occasion, there was no truth on the other side. But then I thought about it further. Though there was no truth to this accusation, it was plausible. I also knew that I had lied in my life—many times in fact—and often not been caught. But here I was being accused of lying when I hadn't, and I was in high dudgeon. It was unfair. I wanted to clear my good name.

Of course, my son was right. There usually is some truth on both sides, even if we have to look beyond the particulars of any given encounter to the larger picture. Spiritually, it is probably a good thing to be falsely accused every once in a while. It helps restore the balance for those times we got away with something, unnoticed by the jury of our peers.

One of my parishioners has perfected a way to deal with such things. Every time someone at work blames him, even for something he was not responsible for, he apologizes. Admittedly, he is a very confident man. But, his tactics have merit. Even in practical terms, much of the time we spend defending ourselves is spent ineffectually. And given what the world's lens does to absolutely everything, it is almost impossible to get the record of our lives absolutely straight. It is certainly impossible to do so at all times with everyone.

Besides, that is not what really matters. All that matters is whether or not we can manage to keep the record of our lives at least somewhat straight with ourselves. If we are at peace with our conscience, what the world thinks about us is secondary. A clear conscience is always free, no matter what the rest of the world may think. By the same token, a guilty conscience transforms even the most smiling, congratulatory world into a prison house, a living hell.

As easily we can be imprisoned by an unnecessarily guilty conscience, turning a lifetime, even a week's worth, of petty evidence against ourselves into a constitutional felony. This serves neither us nor our neighbor. It only serves the futile cause of unhealthy self-absorption. Until we can forgive ourselves for our own humanity, we shouldn't be allowed on any jury that may happen to be trying one of our neighbor's cases. If we tend to be unfairly hard on ourselves, it stands to reason that we will be just as hard on others.

This is why, for most of our crimes I propose a new verdict: "Not guilty by virtue of humanity." Nine out of ten times, this verdict will prove eminently fair. You might even impose this on someone whose case you are trying right now. Before passing judgment, remember this: they are only human too.

"Life I have come to hate,
for what is done under the sun disgusts me."

ECCLESIASTES 2:17

Avoiding judgment is not easy. I think of that young man who sat across from me in my office, fidgeting and avoiding my eyes. I sensed his anger yet couldn't place it. I knew him, but not well. He comes to church most Sundays but doesn't participate in our other activities. I waited for him to speak.

When he finally let his anger loose, he did so with a passion. It was my benediction. He simply couldn't stand my benediction.

I'm accustomed to offending people from the pulpit. Sometimes I even enjoy it. But this was a new one for me, my benediction, the "good words" with which I close every worship service:

And, now, in our going, may God bless and keep us.
May the light of God shine upon us, and out from within us,

68

And be gracious unto us, and bring us peace.
For this is the day we are given.
Let us rejoice and be glad in it.

"You have no right to tell me to rejoice in the days I am given," he said. "No one does."

When this unhappy fellow wandered into my office, I happened to be having a particularly fine day. It's a good thing, too. Such encounters tend to make a bad day worse, and on bad days even I have trouble with my benediction. So I didn't argue, I just listened.

To hear him tell it, his life left almost everything to be desired. Disillusioned in his relationships, his work, and his causes, over the past few months he had built an airtight case against life. This was the day he was given, and he hated it.

He thought he'd found the right woman not so long ago. Their first dates were perfect. A delightful partner, everything she said and did amused, sometimes even inspired him. But lately they'd taken to arguing. Nothing important really, but it shattered his image of her. Their love had faded into an uncomfortable friendship.

At work, the job he'd always dreamed of having, nothing was going as he hoped it would or thought it should. Although he had been on the job only a short time, he found himself longingly casting about for a new position.

And the local peace group to which he gave so much of his time was thrown off balance also—ironically by the end of the cold war—divided down the middle between angry activists and passive pacifists, its energy siphoned off in internecine quarreling.

"I'm disillusioned with everything," he told me. "Even this church. It especially galls me when you tell me to rejoice and be glad, knowing as I do how grim things really are out there."

So I sat there, captive in my own office, smoking my pipe and listening quietly, watching him stare at the floor. Then I remembered something I heard at a peace rally in the late sixties.

"So you're disillusioned," the Reverend William Sloane Coffin had said. "Big deal. All that means is that you were illusioned in the first place."

"For every dream, a vanity to match."

ECCLESIASTES 5:6

Many of our illusions follow on attempts to answer the question, "Why me?" Whether prompted by good or ill fortune, this question brooks no answer. No power, however fervently we pray, orchestrates the random distribution of suffering among life's creatures. This may temper our pride when things are going well, but it lightens our burden when they are not.

A case in point. Suffering some physical or psychological disability ("a painful wound to my pride"), three times the apostle Paul prayed to God to free him from it. God answered, "My grace is all you need; my power finds its full strength in weakness." Humbled into recognizing the dangers of both triumphalism and despair, each a form of pride that estranges us from others, Paul wrote from his prison cell to the church in Philippi, "I have learned, in whatsoever state I am, therewith to be content. I know

71

how to be abased, and I know how to abound: everywhere and in all things I am instructed both to be full and to be hungry, both to abound and suffer need."

In stark contrast, today's culture appears to be spawning a society of victims. Cheered on by lawyers, special interest groups, talk shows, and the tabloids, we are daily encouraged to make sense of our suffering by assigning blame to others. One can measure a trend by its most egregious manifestations. I think of the man who attempted suicide by throwing himself on the subway tracks, only to live and successfully sue New York City for $600,000 damages to requite the pain of his injuries. Or the man who filed a suit against a tobacco company because his wife, who had smoked cigarettes for forty years, died of cancer at the age of sixty-five.

In one respect, all of us are victims. At birth we are bequeathed with family, color, gender, and station in society, none of our own choosing. As part of our inheritance we can be victims of prejudice and misunderstanding, of rules that disadvantage us and benefit others. From that point on, our parents often load us with more baggage than we can easily carry. Lovers betray us. Bosses fire us. Even our friends sometimes flee to escape the clouds over our heads. We get sick. Roofs cave in. Bureaucracies flourish. We are pawns of time and place. The other side of the fence and the right side of the track can betray the expectations of those whose aspirations finally meet fulfillment. We may suffer from want or surfeit, too little or too much attention, too few or too many rules. All of us get hit with storms not of our own making. And even when we are to blame, if we rationalize things properly, we can lay responsibility for our own actions on another's doorstep.

Many self-help books, especially of the therapeutic variety, forgive us for our failures by placing blame elsewhere. They put us in a category (adult child of an alchoholic, incest survivor, battered child, etc.) that explains our own behavior as the inevitable result of a deficient upbringing. Then they promote strategies to enable us to survive our past and enjoy our future.

I respect many parts of the therapeutic agenda. How we think, cope, and behave does stem in part from how we were raised. Every grown-up *is* the adult child of a sometimes childish adult. It helps to understand this, unpack our resentments, and recognize their source. It also helps to isolate and address unhealthy patterns. As Mark Twain observed, "Although the past does not repeat itself, it does rhyme." Besides, having someone to blame besides ourselves can lighten what might otherwise be an unbearable burden. But this can never explain all of life's exigencies. All that our parents are completely responsible for is our birth.

Parents don't have, and never will have, the faintest idea how to raise children blamelessly. However wellintentioned, those who set this as a goal, hoping perhaps to insure that their own children will have nothing negative to report about them to their psychiatrist, are surely the most foolish of all. Parents are human. They make mistakes, sometimes terrible mistakes. Even when they don't, it doesn't require much effort for their grown children to isolate any number of little crimes that add up to a psychological felony. Blaming one's parents for one's own foibles and failures is as easy as shooting fish in a barrel.

When I served as a student chaplain at a mental hospital, I led a daily group session for ten patients. One after another, the participants—schizophrenics, bipolar depressives, addicts—laid the blame for their condition at their parents' doorstep. One member of this group sat for several sessions in silence. Finally, he said, "You know, it's funny. All these years I blamed my failures on the fact that I had no parents. I was an orphan. Listening to you guys, I'm beginning to feel that maybe I was the lucky one."

"A time to break down, and a time to build up."

During the course of a lifetime, all of us suffer shipwrecks. The problem comes when people bring their wrecked ship with them. "See what my parents did to me by putting me into this boat in the first place, or the rocks, or the tides, or my last mapmaker, or the pilot to whom I foolishly entrusted my helm. No longer can I hope to succeed or find happiness, because both have been seized from my grasp." Victimhood is a martyrdom in which no one is saved.

When I use the word *victim*, I am not referring to leaders of groups against whom society discriminates. Those who champion human rights, defending and enhancing the prospects for people suffering discrimination or systemic injustice, are anything but victims. Going back to the Latin root, a victim is one who has been conquered. By refusing to accept vanquishment, either for themselves or the people they defend, reformers—even when they fail or are mistaken in their endeavors—are champions, not victims.

Reformers translate their experience of empathy for the downtrodden into something potentially redemptive. Therapeutic circles serve an equally important healing function. When they transcend the victim mentality, such associations move beyond self-absorption and blame to address strategies for coping with whatever burden their members share. Alcoholics Anonymous and other such groups guide humiliated souls, who have found themselves on the edge of self-destruction, through their own personal midnight to morning. The principles they teach —handing one's life over to a higher power, letting go, taking one day at a time—resonate profoundly with the scriptures, even more so than the teachings of many churches, which can be encumbered with dogma and triumphalism. Even with the righteous anger that follows in the wake of a struggle with inherited demons, pride has no place here. In its stead, the humility that comes from tasting the bitter rind of one's powerlessness, and the supporting community of fellow sufferers, guide people from darkness to a new dawn.

An historical analog from the eighteenth and nineteenth centuries, illustrating both the strengths and limitations of therapeutic communities, is found in the African cults of affliction. Often arising in the wake of epidemics but occasionally in response to colonial repression, communities emerged whose members were bonded together by shared pain. Serving both as an extended kinship group and a therapeutic community, these cults offered opportunities for healing. One cult might consist of people suffering from tuberculosis, another of widows and single mothers, but in every case a common affliction united its members. Utilizing divination and storytelling, their leaders interpreted their common misfortune, thus helping them to come to peace with it.

African cults of affliction offered many of the same services as modern therapeutic associations: community, support, therapy, and insight. Those who participated also became marginalized to a degree, first by setting themselves apart from the society at large, and second, by restricting life's meaning to a single dimension, the affliction shared by the cult members. Yet, shared suffering, even if limited to one particular form of affliction, cultivates the prospect of survival far more than it fosters the spirit of victimhood.

"Slaves I see on horseback,
princes going on foot like slaves."

ECCLESIASTES 10:7

As every victim knows, when dissatisfied with our lot in life we often turn against ourselves or others to apportion blame. This tendency is fostered by the widely shared and extensively marketed belief that people deserve to be happy.

The pursuit of happiness is as American as the Declaration of Independence, where it is codified as a natural right. But Thomas Jefferson, who borrowed these words from the vocabulary of contemporary political thought, had something loftier in mind. For him, the word pursuit meant more a calling than a chase, and happiness—"the greatest good for the greatest number"—something that could only be enjoyed when shared by all. Even so, the right to be happy, as marketed and understood today, is construed more as a matter of individual entitlement than as a code for civil conduct.

The root of our word happiness is "hap," or chance. We hap upon, or chance to encounter, things that give us pleasure. By definition, happiness is a chancy proposition. We may happen to be happy at times, even for long stretches of our lives. But happiness can neither be willed nor permanently sustained.

Compounding many people's sense of dissatisfaction with their own degree of happiness, our self-help culture generally promotes the mixed notion that happiness, though certainly an entitlement available to all, is a state that must be earned by correct behavior. This lends happiness the cachet of a moral attainment: the right to be happy so long as we are good. Born of a positive worldview, namely that we are the masters of our own fate, this Horatio Alger "bootstrap" approach to human destiny has colored much American religion. One finds it in such nineteenth-century oddities as Muscular Christianity, Mind Cure, the Gospel of Relaxation, and the Don't Worry Movement. Today it crops up in Christian Science (a nineteenth-century survivor) and Norman Vincent Peale's power of positive thinking in the 1950s, on into the varied expressions of New Age philosophy. The common signature of all these movements is American optimism, espousing the perfectibility of human nature. Evil, sin, and even disease are unpleasantries that can often be avoided, if only we will live, think, and pray as we ought.

Simplistic cures suggest that to arrive at true happiness, all we have to do is follow a simple set of instructions. "Buy the right map. Get on the suggested path. Stick to it. Follow the numbers. When you arrive at the gate, you will find the key to heaven on earth right in your own pocket. Paradise is yours. Welcome back to the garden. Eat any fruit you like, so long as it isn't fattening. Smile. And have a nice day."

The problem comes when we fail—at love, at work, at life. When knowledge fails, when the abyss of nonbeing and emptiness overwhelms us, all the self-help books in the world, all the happy talk theology of positive thinkers and New Age gurus are next to worthless. Anyone who offers a simple set of steps that we can follow to repair whatever ails us tends only to make us feel more inadequate and incompetent than our neighbors, for not getting right what seems so obvious and easy.

The philosophical underpinning for this sort of thinking lies in the liberal religious tradition, with such exemplars as Ralph Waldo Emerson showing the way. Emerson's theology, generously drawn and non-dogmatic, has much to commend it. Yet he contributed directly to the tradition of sovereign individualism, which may ennoble us when things are going well, but leaves us stranded when we need the comfort and aid of others to sustain us. Touting the value of self-reliance, Emerson argued that as individuals we are responsible for our own destiny. He taught that within ourselves, where the oversoul abides, we can find all the resources we will need to thrive in life. Whenever we experience something painful or difficult, all we have to do is respond with strength, and proverbially, we will not only overcome the obstacle but build our character as well.

This is a myth. When it works, when we recover from failure, grief, or pain through our own efforts alone, we only get tougher and harder, more armored, better defended, less vulnerable. This may sound appealing, but it actually cuts us off from others rather than bridging our isolation and loneliness to some source that will allay them. And that is when self-reliance works. Often it does not.

My grandmother, born in Idaho in 1888, was fond of saying that we can't understand what another person is feeling unless we have walked a mile in his or her moccasins. Pain resonates with pain, suffering with suffering. People who suppress their own suffering can attempt to comfort others. Tracing the word back to its root meaning, they can be "with them in strength." But only rarely can they commiserate, "share their misery" or console them, be "one with them in their aloneness." Until we are broken, plunged into our own tragic depths and strangeness, another's pain will remain outside our immediate experience. This will spare us grief. It will also fail to offer another the consolation he or she deserves.

Contrast this with Ralph Waldo Emerson's aversion to any kind of dependence. His philosophy deepened with age and loss, but as a young man, when he wrote his most influential works, Emerson refused to sully himself by assuming any personal responsibility for another's feelings or actions. In his essay "Self-Reliance," Emerson wrote that, "Discontent is the want of self-reliance; it is infirmity of will. Our sympathy is just as base. . . . Nothing can bring you peace but yourself." Adopting a popular term from contemporary therapeutic literature, we encounter what might be called "counter-dependency" (or "sovereign independence"), the perfect solution for every human entanglement. But we must reckon the cost. Self-reliance may insulate us from suffering, but it also liberates us from the pain and privilege of a shared humanity.

As American philosopher William James asked—*after* he had rejected suicide—"Let us see whether pity, pain, and fear, and the sentiment of human helplessness may not open a profounder view and put into our hands a more complicated key to meaning."

*"Woe to the man by himself with no one
to help him up when he falls down."*

ECCLESIASTES 4:10

Moving beyond self-reliance to connect with others, especially through confession of our own failures and pain, can change both our lives and theirs.

I know a woman whom everyone, especially the members of her family, considered a complete success. A perfect mother, wife, and daughter; a powerful, remarkably successful lawyer—she had it all. What they didn't know she one day confessed to me. Her life was torture. She lived in daily pain, fearful that her self-destructive secret life might be discovered—her multiple affairs, her loneliness, her profound sense of unworthiness. Until then she had maintained perfect pretense. In truth, brilliant and successful as it appeared, her life was a shambles.

She earnestly wished to break the pattern, end her empty marriage, and "come out" as a flawed and broken person but remained terrified that, if she did, her friends and family would reject her. Finally, she couldn't endure the pretense any longer. In full detail, she confessed to her parents and sisters the wreck her life had become, praying for their support and understanding. She received more than she prayed for. For the first time in all their years together, her family felt able to share their own pain and insecurities with her. They could finally risk this, because they knew that she would empathize. She wouldn't judge them severely for being less than perfect themselves. A whole system of family neuroses, boxes within boxes, finally began to be unpacked. True bonds of sympathy replaced the yoke of pretense that before had held the family together while keeping its members apart.

There is nothing surprising here. Failure strips our lives of pretense. It forces us to realize that we are not in charge. We need every ounce of help we can get, not only to make it through tough times but to rejoice along the way. Our failures unite us with others, who then can admit without fear of judgment that they too have failed.

*"The race does not go to the swift,
nor the battle to the strong."*

ECCLESIASTES 9:11

This woman and her family learned that to accept ourselves and forgive others, sometimes the best route is to turn a weakness into a strength. We enter here the realm of paradox.

Someone once asked Catholic monk Thomas Merton, perhaps the most provocative spiritual teacher of our time, to contribute to a book on success. What made him successful, the editor asked. What advice might he offer others on their road to success? Merton responded with magnificent impertinence: "Be anything you like, be madmen, drunks, and bastards of every shape and form, but at all costs avoid one thing: success." Merton is speaking in the language of paradox. To find meaning in affliction such a language often is required, one that turns things upside down and inside out.

In mathematics and logic, a paradox is a puzzle that cannot be solved by conventional proof. As such, paradoxes serve an important function. They stretch the framework in which we contemplate the nature of reality.

Christian paradox is grounded in the teaching of Jesus ("the last shall be first"; "empty yourself and be filled"; "lose yourself and be found") but also in the letters of Paul, who no less often enlists paradox to open the sacred envelope. "As dying, and, behold, we live," Paul writes of his fellow Christians. "As sorrowful, yet always rejoicing. As poor, yet making many rich. As having nothing, and yet possessing all things." Of himself Paul says, "When I am weak, then am I strong."

One modern Christian master of paradox is the Danish philosopher Søren Kierkegaard. He isolated two forms of willfulness, describing each almost to perfection, since he struggled so profoundly in his own life with both. One is this. Dependent on no one, self-actualized individuals vainly attempt to liberate themselves from everything that lies outside their own control. Welcome to the dark essence of humanism. Man or woman attempts to become God.

The second form of willfulness—the flip side of pride —presents a perfect negative print, despair, which Kierkegaard named "the sickness unto death." In despair, "eternity puts thee under arrest by thyself," he wrote. Despair is self-hating pride. You are hurting. Life has turned against you. So what do you do? You exclude the rest of creation and wallow in your pain as if no one else before or beside you had ever failed, fallen, or grieved.

86

Kierkegaard wanted to escape from his own aloneness, which he painted as poignantly as anyone ever has, but he refused. He could not stop being alone. He took an existential leap and fell into the arms of God, but no one else was there and so God couldn't catch him. Yet one thing Kierkegaard understood, striving throughout his life to teach himself, is that we can be saved only when we are lost. This fits into the classic frame of Christian paradox. In the words of Martin Luther, "Only those who are sick require the doctor; only the sheep that is lost is looked for; only the captive is freed; only the poor is enriched; only the weak is made strong; only the humble is exalted; only what is empty is filled; only what is scattered can be assembled."

Confronted with such contrarian logic, one must choose between the paradoxical wisdom of Jesus, Paul, Kierkegaard, Luther, Lao Tse, and many others, and the rational heritage of Aristotle. Aristotle is the great-grandfather of all who pride themselves on their critical faculties, rationality, and scientific methodology. He coined something called the law of the excluded middle. Put in lay terms, something cannot be both hot and not-hot at the same time. That is to say, if something is hot it can't be cold. It makes sense. We cannot be early if we are late. We cannot be rich if we are poor. We cannot be first if we are last. We cannot know joy when our lives are darkened by sorrow.

According to Jesus, none of this is true.

"Do not be over-virtuous
nor play too much the sage."

No story in any sacred canon is more riddled with paradox than the story of Jesus. Jesus taught
that only the sinner, the prostitute, the prodigal, stands
much of a chance of being saved. He dismissed the upright and exalted the downtrodden. He answered hate
with love and gained his final victory on a cross.

By any conventional reckoning, Jesus was a failure.
His disciples believed he would march into Jerusalem
and ascend to David's rightful throne as scion and mes-
siah. Instead, he was betrayed by one of his own disciples
and crucified between two thieves.

"I thirst," he cried. "Father, why hast thou forsaken
me?" He forgives his enemies, sighs "It is finished," and
then dies. His followers scatter. Everyone who believed
in him, with the telling exception of his beloved disciple

John, and the three women (Mary Magdalene, Salome, and Mary, the mother of James) who attended to his body and stood vigil at his tomb, failed.

Especially Peter failed. Just before he died, Jesus passed his keys to Peter: Peter who fell asleep when Jesus asked him to stand guard as he prayed. Peter whose ignorance led Jesus to shout, "Get thee behind me, Satan." Peter who, in fear and panic, betrayed Jesus three times, disowning any knowledge of him. Peter the weak. Peter the failure. Saint Peter the rock on whom Christ built his church.

Perhaps the most paradoxical of Jesus' teachings, something new in the canons of religious literature, is that we should love our enemies. He didn't pose this in terms of love and hate. He didn't go on to say love casts out hate. He said love casts out fear. He said that God is love, that we should love our neighbors as ourselves, and that love to God and love to neighbor sum up all the law and the commandments.

Think about how the pieces fit together. If the opposite of love is fear, fear looms as an impediment to every kind of love—personal, neighborly, and divine.

Following Jesus' logic, an enemy is someone we fear. We may also hate him but unless we fear him, he does not really have power over us, not power over our heart. This is as true of our late fear of the Soviet Union as it is of our fear of another individual. Since love casts out fear, loving our enemies accomplishes two useful things. It diminishes their power over us and liberates our soul from fear.

Fear, on the other hand, sets up a protective shield. This shield does not protect us from our enemies as intended; it only protects us from ourselves. Since the opposite of love is not hate but fear, all that fear finally protects us from is the possibility of love.

Though we don't often view it in these terms, we may accept fear's logic because we need, or sense we need, protection from love. Forget about your enemies. Loving enemies is material for a much more advanced course in spiritual discipline. Think about your attempts to love those who are struggling to love you in return.

To nurture and sustain a loving relationship we must conquer the fears that induce self-protection. Self-protection seems user-friendly, yet all it does is close us off from others. Self-protection veils our hearts. Even more sadly it may armor them.

Think of how often in our closest relationships surface irritations create a climate of anger or distance. One and then both partners or loved ones hold on to their sense of grievance long after the cause is forgotten. And then consider, if I may be perverse for a moment, how convenient this is. It permits us to close our hearts. Why is that convenient? Because a closed heart locks in both directions. Grudges or any well-practiced pattern of avoidance or confrontation not only keep another out, they also keep us from having to encounter the source of our own fears.

When Jesus says that we should love our neighbors as ourselves, it is sobering to remember that most of us don't love ourselves, not really. I suspect that one reason we tend to avoid deep self-examination (something essential for any kind of meaningful spiritual growth) is that we are afraid of what we will discover and would prefer not dealing with it, because it is too painful.

Almost every kind of fear is a fear of pain, our own pain and our loved one's pain as well. A fear of pain may drive us to hide behind work or drink or almost any blinds convenient to us. It also may drive us to try to eliminate others' pain, to deny it, or even to blame them for it, as if their pain were somehow a symbol of failure rather than an expression of honest, often profound feeling. Until we can muster the courage to accept, even embrace our own and others' pain, fear will be our master and love its victim.

I think of a couple I once knew. The husband professed to love his wife unconditionally. He would do anything for her. All he wanted was for her to be happy. Above all else, he wished her to be free from pain. On the surface this might strike you as solicitous behavior. Far from it. The reason he couldn't stand his wife's pain is that her unhappiness threatened and excluded him. He took it personally. He blamed himself for her pain, shifting attention from her to his own culpability. This pattern, which triggered her own fears, intensified until even the slightest altercation or miscommunication could lead to a terrible scene.

We may even blame our loved ones for their pain. I once counseled a woman who was furious with her husband for having cancer. She didn't admit to this, but that was what it was. His sickness threw a stone into the well-protected surface of her life, and she was unprepared for the ripples. This left her frightened of the future, suddenly insecure without the guarantee of his accustomed presence and support. Because she handled his sickness and its consequences poorly, she blamed her husband for it. She blamed him for his pain and for introducing the specter of pain into her life.

So not only does our fear of enemies provoke us into putting up a self-protective shield. We put up such a shield even against our loved ones. The reason fear casts out love is that we cannot love when our heart is protected by a shield. Fear may appear to protect us from pain by protecting us from the feelings of others, feelings over which we sometimes have no control. But by the same token, this same fear casts out love, because we cannot love unless we honor others' feelings, unless we walk toward their pain and through our own.

To sustain love is difficult but not complicated. The secret is this. We care enough about another to stop being driven by our own fears: fears of intimacy or self-revelation, fears of confrontation, in fact fear of any of the myriad masks pain can wear. When we dare to risk pain—our own, another's, the pain we share—love casts out fear. That's how it works. Love casts out fear, and pain becomes manageable, a part of life and not nearly the most dominant part. Most important of all, when we walk toward our pain, not away from it, we walk hand in hand with others, hesitant sometimes but no longer fearful, for love is strong, strong enough to cast fear from our hearts.

This is not eros that casts out our fear of pain. It is agape. Not romantic love, but something much more universal and redemptive, something that saves us and others from ourselves, something much more like the love of God.

"Better wisdom than warlike weapons."

ECCLESIASTES 9:18

God is our name for that which is greater than all and yet present in each, a symbol for ultimate value, the sign we follow in our search for transcendent worth. When we pray to God, we are asking our deepest, truest voice to make itself heard.

Does prayer work? If by prayer we mean asking God to intervene to give us something we want, the answer is "No, prayer doesn't work." One needn't stretch to prove this. Can you even begin to imagine how many prayers have been offered in vain over the past decade in response to the AIDS tragedy? "Please, God, let my test turn out negative." "Please, God, don't let her die. I'll do anything, if only you let her live." Does prayer work? In the hard light of experience, if this is what we mean by prayer, it does not.

Our English word *prayer* stems from the Latin verb *precari*, to entreat or beg. Another offshoot of the same root is the word *precarious*. Precarious means "obtained by entreaty" and therefore undependable.

Prayer is undependable. Sometimes the test turns out negative; sometimes it doesn't. Sometimes she recovers; sometimes she dies.

People who believe that God weighs our prayers in the balance and then votes yea or nay get both themselves and God into trouble. The most influential Unitarian minister of the twentieth century, A. Powell Davies, left the Methodist church after a tiff with one such person. A member of his congregation told the young minister that her son had been the only survivor of a naval ship torpedoed in the North Sea because she prayed for him every night. Davies exploded like a Roman candle. "Do you actually believe," he asked incredulously, "that God let two hundred boys die because their *mothers* were insufficiently pious?"

Though he doesn't go on to record it, I can imagine how this confrontation might have continued.

"The Bible does teach, sir, that one with sufficient faith can move mountains."

"In this respect, madam, the Bible is an ass."

"How can you call yourself a man of God if you reject God's word?"

"Your God is not love, madam. Your God is worse than Santa Claus, distributing gifts only to children whose mothers have been good."

Twelve years ago, when the late Chuck Weiss and I founded the AIDS Task Force at All Souls Church, we acted in the same spirit that moved Powell Davies to become a Unitarian minister. We were responding to the simplistic, divisive, and profoundly unchristian notion that AIDS was God's punishment for immoral behavior. We both knew that if God is anywhere, God is certainly by the bedside of those who suffer, suffering with them, loving them, certainly not condemning them, not compounding their pain. But we also knew something else, something in its own way just as hard to reckon with. We knew that God was not answering our prayers and theirs. "Please, let the test turn out negative. Please, don't let him die. Please shine your light on the way to a cure."

As long as we picture God as a combination Santa Claus and criminal court judge, our attempts to decipher God's will or curry God's favor will be both trivial and vain. That doesn't mean there is no God. Or that prayer doesn't work. It simply means that some things are beyond both our power and God's to effect or change.

One of the reasons I believe in God more deeply than I did ten years ago is that I have witnessed manifestations of the holy where I hitherto might least have expected to encounter it. Some of the most spiritual people I know, many of them members and late members of my congregation, are or were living with AIDS. But that's just it: *living* with AIDS, not dying from AIDS. What makes or made their living spiritual is what makes all of our living spiritual, an appreciation for life as a gift rather than a given: an understanding of life as a bittersweet sacrament to be partaken of and shared with reverence, compassion, and, at moments of deepest communion, profound joy.

This is also where prayer fits in, where it does work. Prayer doesn't change things that can't be changed. Prayer helps give us the strength and insight to change things that can, like our hearts, or even our lives.

Let me give you an example, at once simple and difficult. You are estranged from someone who is or was once close to you. Between you has grown up a thicket of anger, bitterness, recrimination. You may even hate one another, only because you care so deeply. (We rarely waste anger and bitterness on people whose attitudes toward us don't matter.) You are trapped in your own estrangement. Its thorns pierce your soul.

So what do you do? You find a quiet place, where you will not be interrupted. You close your eyes. And you pray for this person. First you picture his face in your mind. Then you remember that he too will die, that everything between you will soon pass, that the universe will fold you both back into her bosom. Picture his face in your mind and pray for him.

"Dear God, may he find some peace in his soul. May he know you and the joy that comes from knowing you before he dies. May the sun shine upon him and brighten his life. May he be released from some of his pain. May he find your love in his heart."

Let me tell you something. I am sure that this is true. It is impossible to hate someone and pray for him or her at the same time. Does this change them? Does it unlock their heart and turn their anger away from you? Does God listen to your prayer for them and then wave a magic wand over their head? No, of course not. God listens to your prayer for them and then waves a magic wand over *your* head. You change. You are free, if but for a time, from the thicket. Your prayer pulls the thorns from your own heart.

And then the world changes. Each change of heart changes the world. This is how forgiveness works as well. When we forgive someone we don't change her, but ourselves. We liberate ourselves from all obligation to continuing bitterness. This doesn't reverse the past. It doesn't remove from the record whatever crime was perpetrated against us. But it changes the present and the future.

Now, what happens the next time you see the person who has hurt you? If you have prayed for him, what you see when you look into his eyes will change. It will temper your fear. Remember, at least some of the thorns have been pulled out. His power over you in part is determined by your need to recriminate, to hurt in kind. Your change of heart—not of mind—may reverse the cycle of self-protective vindictiveness that holds you in thralldom to one another.

I am speaking of you and your father. Or you and your daughter, or your wife, or ex-husband, or boss, or an estranged friend. No amount of anger or bitterness will protect you from the pain they may inflict on your life.

On the contrary. But if you pray for them, you may discover a bond of kinship that will replace your other bonds. Your heart is lightened. Your pain is lessened, and with your pain, your fear.

And this is the hardest kind of prayer.

"A time for keeping silent,
a time for speaking."

ECCLESIASTES 3:7

Self-acceptance and forgiveness finally are the same. Each connects us with others. And without them our lifelines will not hold. This is true even of our most casual encounters.

I have a friend who always complained whenever I asked him how he was.

"How are you?" I would ask.

"Terrible," he would reply. "My back is a mess, and last week my neck went out. All of which is only slightly less disconcerting than the bill I just got from my urologist."

Not that he was exaggerating. A youthful sixty in aspiration and energy, he has cut out tennis, which he loves, and missed his vacation last year, confined to bed with a back that wouldn't work.

When I ask a person how she or he is, I don't really expect an honest answer. "How are you?" is like "Hello," the sort of greeting we offer to passing acquaintances when we are running late for an appointment. With this man it was different. He almost always answered truthfully. So you can imagine my surprise when I ran into him on the street recently and asked him how he was.

"Fine," he said.

I was in a hurry, but this caught me up short. Stopping in the middle of the sidewalk, I pulled him into a doorway and said, "What did you say?"

"I'm fine."

"What do you mean you're fine? Last week you had a brace on your neck, and today you're walking with a limp."

"Let me tell you something," he replied. "It took me years, but I finally got the message. Whatever may be wrong with me, most people tell me they're worse off than I am. If you don't believe me, when someone asks you, 'How you are?' just dare say, 'My neck hurts,' or 'My back aches.' Chances are you won't get commiseration; you'll get one-upmanship. You'll have to suffer through hearing about the other person's neck, back, anything that directs attention and sympathy to him. Most people can't seem to empathize, only compete. So I've made up my mind. Starting this week, when I'm asked how I am, I'm going to say, 'Fine.'

"All this got me thinking," he continued. "You know my doctors never complain about how they feel. It's not their job. Their job is to make others feel better. And it's not a bad job, when you think about it. So you know what I'm going to do with the rest of my life? I'm going to empathize with people in pain. I feel that pain. I know how much it hurts. And I know for certain that they have as hard a time as I do getting that across."

"How are you going to do this?" I asked.

"I'm never again going to say, 'How are you?' when I don't really want to know. And when I do want to know, I'm going to ask, 'Are you okay?' For some reason, when you put it that way, people tend to be honest. And when they start to tell me how bad off they are, I'm not going to compete with them, just listen. Even if they're better off than I am. And then I will tell them how terrible it sounds. And they will feel a little better."

"What about you?" I asked.

"I will feel a little better, too."

PART III

Compassion & Humility: Lifelines to God & Our Neighbors

"Vanity of vanities. All is vanity."

It is 5:20 in the morning. You are dreaming
that last strange dream of the night, flying from one
room to another, soaring higher and higher. It is exhila-
rating yet strange, strange and then frightening. You
cannot stop. Up and up you go, beyond the top of the
building, through scaffolding and I-beams. And then
you fall. You hit the ground (your bedroom floor), awakened by the blow—books, lamps, your television flying
through the air. You must be dreaming, but you are not
dreaming. You have fallen. The world is shaking. You
grab a blanket, run from your apartment down the stairs,
stairs overridden with naked or half-clothed neighbors,
screaming. You flee into the street, into a nightmare more
real than any dream, fires framing black silhouetted
buildings, buckled pavement, no lights, no sirens, only
muffled human cries.

One week later: five thousand dead, tens of thousands injured, homeless, each bereft by unimaginable loss—the loss of parents and children, of lovers, sisters, and brothers—victims of nature, a savage and indiscriminate god.

So what about God? Was God's hand involved in the Kobe earthquake? It's unconscionable to think so, but we have to pose the question. It's the question we always ask when tragedy strikes.

The question we ask is *why*. Why is the thirty-seven-year-old daughter-in-law of a member of my congregation dying of ovarian cancer? Why did five children in Queens, New York, perish in a recent fire? Why did a tornado pick worship hour on Sunday morning to hit a church in South Carolina, killing the minister's four-year-old daughter? What had he done to anger God? Don't you think he asked himself that question? Better to have asked, what had she done, or her hundreds of little brothers and sisters in Kobe, to deserve so untimely and brutal a sentence of death.

A Christian pastor who lost his faith when his young wife died in childbirth once said to me, "If God exists, then God is a bastard." If God is omniscient and omnipotent—all-knowing and all-powerful—then God knows when we are going to die and how. Not only that, but should God choose to do so, God also has the power to change the course of human destiny, to spare this woman, to stop the ovens, to hold the earth's plates together at the line of fissure. Such a God is not love. Such a God is the deus ex machina of Kobe and Auschwitz, of both natural and unnatural, both inhuman and inhumane catastrophe. Conversely, if God is *not* omniscient and omnipotent, by orthodox Christian reckoning at least, God is not God.

To this extent, I am an atheist. I am an atheist when it comes to Kobe and Auschwitz. My heart tells me that there is no God pushing the buttons and pulling the strings, permitting the ovens to incinerate innocents, shaking the earth, killing our children. When anyone takes the Bible and tries to explain away something like the earthquake in Kobe, I open it and say with the Preacher in Ecclesiastes, "The fate of the sons of men and the fate of beasts is the same; as one dies so dies the other. . . . All go to one place; all are from the dust, and all turn to dust again." And should anyone dare employ the Bible to justify God's ways to the men, women and children lining up for the showers of Auschwitz, I again quote the Preacher: "[I have seen] all the oppressions that are practiced under the sun. And behold, the tears of the oppressed, and they had no one to comfort them."

When tragedy strikes, the question is not "why did this happen?" or "what did we do to deserve this?" Rarely do we deserve death, our own or our loved ones'. But this is only half the human equation, for none of us did anything to deserve life either. Death and life come wrapped in the same strange package. Life is a gift, undeserved, unexpected, one might even say a gift from God.

So I am an atheist in this respect only: I cannot believe in the God that many others seem to believe in. This God is too small, too petty and capricious, unequal to the mixed and manifold abundance of the creation. I cannot believe in a God who keeps records and makes lists. I can't believe in a God who has an Auschwitz department or a Kobe department in his vast cosmic bureaucracy. But I also know, as someone once said of people who don't believe in God, it's not that they therefore believe in nothing. They tend to believe in almost anything. Most of the things they believe in are even smaller than the God I don't believe in. Money. Fame. Success. Knowledge. "All are vanity."

The word vain carries two complementary connotations: puffed up and empty (or impossible). To elevate ourselves above others is vanity, because from dust we all come and to dust we shall return; and attempting to do what cannot be done or to know what cannot be known is a vain, or impossible, endeavor. In common parlance, vanity is pride. We cannot form saving connections when we permit pride to distance us from others. And when we tether our hopes to a vain object, our lifelines will not hold. On the other hand, compassion unites us with others, and humility concedes our human limitations.

One of the smallest things we believe in when we don't believe in God is ourselves. After the last earthquake in Los Angeles, the engineers and architects in Japan proudly proclaimed to their people that a like devastation could never happen there, for they had designed and girded their buildings and bridges to endure nature's wrath. They believed in themselves. That is why pride is so great a sin, the greatest sin of all. No other human presumption so perilously exposes us to the whiplash of reality.

Since most people who call themselves atheists show their pride by vesting their rationality with sovereign authority, though the little God they disbelieve in is no different than the little God I disbelieve in, I am really not an atheist, not as they claim to be. Unlike them, I believe in what I cannot know, the God beyond God, not omnipotent and omniscient—these are human constructs—but ineffable and inscrutable, subject neither to human description nor human understanding. When I say I believe in God, God is not God's name. God is our name for that which is greater than all and yet present in each, a mystery that cannot be named or known.

None of this makes sense. I know that. By definition, a thing we can neither name nor know cannot possibly make sense. That is the trouble with God. The trouble with us begins when we cannot accept this, or when we try to explain for ourselves or to others what cannot be understood. We also get in trouble when we imagine that nothing exists beyond that which we can in fact understand and explain. Finally, we get in trouble when we allow what little we know to get in the way of our relationship with our neighbors, given that our knowledge of the ineffable and inscrutable cannot be that much greater than theirs.

If none of this makes sense, it does make something more important than sense. It makes us humble. And it makes us wonder. It helps us empathize with others as mysteriously born and as fated to die as we are. It puts us and our vanity in perspective. It humbles us, and we are changed.

Humbled, we recognize and accept that life is undeserved, fragile, sometimes painful, ultimately unpredictable, and certainly unfathomable. We are changed when, acknowledging this and embracing it, we no longer demand of life or God more than either can deliver: answers to the question *why*.

*"Even if the man had lived a thousand years twice over
. . . does not he go to the same place?"*

ECCLESIASTES 6:6

In each of our lives the boom will one day fall.
Maybe we lower it on ourselves, brooding through a long,
dark winter of reflection and struggle, our old familiar
lights having finally flickered out. Maybe a parent dies, or
a spouse or child. Maybe we are fired or rejected, or fail
in a way that the world, at least that part of the world closest to our heart, cannot help but notice and condemn.
Maybe we hit bottom, one too many drink to our long
since exhausted credit. Maybe our doctor gives us three
months to live.

Whatever happens to precipitate a crisis in our lives,
one temptation is to hunker down, to rely on our own
strength to get us through. This has ancient precedent in
the Greek mythological tradition. Even today, the most
familiar metaphor for someone who emerges from fail-

ure or despair to thrive again is phoenix springing from the ashes.

In his book *Metamorphoses*, a compendium of ancient religious mythology, Ovid traces the phoenix story to Assyria, where legend tells of a bird that gives birth to itself when it dies. The historian Herodotus, admitting reliance on pictures rather than personal experience, describes the phoenix in these words: "Part of his plumage is gold-colored, and part crimson; and he is for the most part very much like an eagle in outline and bulk." This regal, solitary bird lives for five hundred years on a diet of frankincense, a fragrant resin; then, when death approaches, it gathers cinnamon and myrrh and with them builds a nest high in the branches of an oak tree. As it expires, a new phoenix rises from its body, emerging on the wings of its final breath.

In other embellishments of this legend, the myrrh is fashioned in the shape of an egg around the dying phoenix. As the carcass rots, a worm emerges from the moldering flesh, and feeds on the carcass within this sweet putrefying egg until the shell of myrrh cracks and the phoenix is born anew. According to Tacitus, the young phoenix then "collects a quantity of myrrh, and to try its strength makes frequent excursions with a load on its back. When he has gained sufficient confidence in his own vigor, he takes up the body of his father and flies with it to the altar of the Sun, where he leaves it to be consumed in flames of fragrance." Returning to earth the phoenix then lives another span of five hundred years, and the cycle repeats itself. Possessing eagle- and anchorite-like courage and living on a diet of perfumes and divine vapors, the phoenix is unlike any other creature, completely self-sufficient, self-actualizing, and self-created. In the story of the phoenix, dust to dust and ashes to ashes is transfigured from the ultimate argument for humility to grounds for pride, the dust uncommon and the ashes sweet.

In Buddhism, Bodhisattvas deny themselves Nirvana, returning to suffer with and for others until all suffering has ceased. In Christianity, Christ dies that others may attain eternal life. In contrast, the phoenix dies unto and for himself, gives birth to himself, collects his strength, and develops courage to honor himself. Even as the eagle is the most solitary and regal of birds, the gold and crimson phoenix, whose manna is not milk and honey but odoriferous gums and perfumes, constitutes the perfect icon for the crest of nineteenth-century existentialist philosopher Friedrich Nietzsche's superman, his shield lifted in defiance of the fates, his spirit undaunted and unvanquished by the pathos of human mortality.

"There is nothing new under the sun."

Nietzsche and the phoenix shared the same aspiration: to rise beyond their fellows and soar. In this respect, Nietzsche is the unnamed patron saint of the modern human-potential movement. As he did, most human-potential or self-realization schools, loosely classified under the New Age rubric, promise the possibility of individual enlightenment through the attainment of special knowledge.

The New Age offers real attractions. No matter what the teaching, spiritual circles of like-minded seekers invite intimacy. They also provide comfort, if often only for a weekend at a time, and outlets for the sharing of mutual concerns. In contrast, mainstream churches (including my own) can appear sterile and impersonal. Most appealingly, at least for Americans accustomed to having choices in everything, New Age writers and movements offer something for everybody. From *The Celestine Prophecy* by James Redfield to the Church of Scientology, people can experiment with a rich, even bewildering, variety of paths to meaning, consolation, and knowledge.

Following in the footsteps of ancient Gnostics (*gnosis* being the Greek word for knowledge), New Age teachers promise peace of mind as the reward for those who decode the secrets of the cosmos. In most instances, individuals must discover this knowledge within themselves. They may employ meditation, channeling, crystal talismans, some guru's "higher truth," or the discovery of past lives. With light the dominant symbol, darkness is often understood as a chimera that appears real only to the unknowing eye. The same is sometimes said of evil and death.

Some New Age guides offer wisdom well worth pondering. Among recent bestsellers, I think of Robert Bly's *Iron John* and Clarissa Pinkola Estes's *Women Who Run with the Wolves*. Presenting a deft mixture of psychology and legend, these thoughtful mytho-poetic psychological teachers call us to rise from our subservience to the demigods of the modern ethos (such as materialism, conformism, and sexism). Attempting to rewrite and recover the human soul map from traditional religious ownership, these post-Christian spiritual guidebooks serve a useful purpose. Coupling modern and ancient interpretive mediums (including Jungian, Freudian, and Maslovian psychiatry; Greek mythology; Arthurian legend; and Native American folklore), the literature tapped here provides insights that conventional religious writings, or the usual secular fare, fail to deliver. The more varied our psychic landscape, the richer our possibilities for spiritual refreshment. Religious syncretism, the mixing of stories or ideas from different traditions, can create a powerful synthesis. The history of Judaism and Christianity is replete with generative moments of cross-pollination, from fields as widespread as Sumerian theology, Greek ethics, and Islamic philosophy.

Yet the underlying message of contemporary mythopoetic literature is troubling to me. One might sum it up as follows: "You are in pain. It is someone else's fault, especially society's. It is also your fault, because you have it in your power to escape it, first by naming (the knowledge piece), second by rejecting (the power piece), and finally by setting yourself free (the liberation piece). Then you will be everything you are not now: strong, vital, grounded, independent, wise, and—since you would not wish to forget the rest of us—nurturing, caring, sustaining and loving, insofar as you are loved."

I call this literature neo-Nietszchean, because, like Nietszche, most of these new prophets challenge us to lift ourselves beyond the confines of common human existence, to thrive where others languish, to liberate ourselves from the sorry lot of our brothers and sisters by refusing to accept conventional limitations imposed on the human spirit. The human condition becomes something to escape in an act of human will, not to accept as a fact of human birth.

When I was an adolescent I read almost everything Nietszche wrote and loved it all. I can still remember the rush I felt when I encountered his liberating message. I could free myself from the bondage of convention and climb with Zarathustra to the mountaintop. With Bible stories identified in my mind with my sleepy Presbyterian church in Boise, Idaho, Nietzsche fed my spiritual hunger with panache, tapping Greek myth, in all its aloof Apollonian and vibrant Dionysiac glory, to counter the conventions of Christianity.

In Nietzsche's opinion, Christianity cultivated a culture of weak, repressed, submissive people. "Blessed are the meek, for they shall inherit the earth. Blessed are they who mourn, for they shall be comforted." Don't be meek, he countered. Don't mourn. Be free, independent, and strong. For an adolescent, it's a winning message. And he didn't challenge only Christianity, for the fundamental teachings of Buddhism tap the same vein. Buddhism teaches that life is filled with grief and suffering and ends in death. Life's saving essence is not freedom or happiness but compassion. And compassion evolves only as a result of shared suffering, through a growing appreciation for the nature of human existence. The Buddhist and Christian approaches to suffering are different. Yet both find the compassion that emerges in response to suffering to be central to human growth. In contrast, disdain for compassion as a weak virtue set the tone for Nietszche's rebellion.

Nietszche's superman broke through society's constraints in order to attain his full humanity. Beyond good and evil, liberated from repressive religious conventions that encouraged weakness in order to maintain control, the radical, liberated individual read his or (less often) her own soul map, followed it, and found power in freedom. The arrogance of Nietszche's superman, who would have despised Hitler's subordination of the individual to a quasi-religious state mythos, proved so alluring that with a little bit of accommodation he served as a perfect prototype for the Third Reich.

For some individuals, neo-Nietzschean teachings can be therapeutic. But they also beguile the follower into believing that if only he or she, combining knowledge with power, could free the real man or wild woman within, liberation would follow. This is ennobling in the abstract. But to teach that such an ideal is attainable diminishes our tolerance for the less-than-ideal lives we inevitably have. Human suffering is not only born of imperfect knowledge, flawed families, bondage to convention, lack of spiritual insight, racism and sexism, poverty, or repressive religious or ideological hegemony. It is born of birth and ends with death.

Those who promise meaning through the attainment of higher knowledge create another problem. By individualizing enlightenment and placing human salvation or self-actualization outside the context of the larger community, they flatter their adherents into a posture of spiritual elitism. More sensitive men and stronger women work out together in a wide range of spiritual fitness centers, but each on his or her own machine. Even as health clubs and organic food centers offer physical well-being as an antidote to aging and death, these New Age spiritual alternatives to conventional religion promise much the same—hard work perhaps, but also a means to elevate ourselves above others.

The Catholic theologian John S. Dunne offers a cautionary lesson, the parable of the mountain. One day a group of spiritual seekers begins to climb a mountain in search of enlightenment. God, they are told, lives at the top of this mountain. So they leave their daily cares behind them and climb in hope of meeting God and receiving divine knowledge. Finally, they reach the peak of the mountain. From this lofty promontory they can see farther than they have ever seen before. And the air is thin at the top of the mountain. This is conducive to abstract and disembodied reflection on the eternal verities, the very things that are confounded and veiled by the grossness, busyness, and squalor of the all-too-human life below. There is only one problem. God is not there. While they were climbing up the mountain in search of enlightenment, God was climbing down the mountain into the valley. As the pilgrims in quest of transfiguration seek escape from the limitations of their human lot, God is by the bedside of the dying, comforting those who mourn, forgiving those who fail, consoling those who suffer.

According to this parable, God is not knowledge, God is love.

"No one can master the wind to hold it back."

For those of us who believe that God is love,
the most troubling question anyone can ask is "Why does
evil then exist?" Why do innocent people suffer such terrible affliction? How could God ignore or even set in
motion the wanton destruction inflicted by a deranged
bomber or an earthquake? Every religious tradition offers insights into darkness, yet few texts, scriptural or
otherwise, probe the question of theodicy—the vindica-
tion of God from responsibility for evil—more search-
ingly than the Book of Job.

Job's story is familiar. In the court of heaven, God asks
his prosecuting attorney, Satan, where he has been.
"Ranging over the earth from end to end," Satan replies.
According to the Book of Job, Satan and God are on the
same team. Playing bad cop to God's good cop, Satan fer-
rets out wrongdoing and brings it to God's attention.

Taunting Satan, God asks, "Have you considered my servant Job? You will find no one like him on earth, a man of blameless and upright life, who fears God and sets his face against wrongdoing."

Satan could not be less impressed. Job has every reason to be God-fearing. Wealthy, free of troubles, and blessed with a large and happy family, how could he complain, having no earthly complaints? Take all that away, "and he will curse you to your face." Rising to the bait, God challenges Satan to strip Job of all he has, save only his life. Thus begin the trials and passion of Job.

The Sabaeans, nomads from Arabia, invade and plunder Job's estate, killing his herdsman and stealing his flock. Then his children attend a party, a whirlwind strikes, the roof collapses, and all beneath it die. For a time Job maintains his composure, philosophical in his resignation: "Naked I came from the womb, naked I shall return whence I came. The Lord giveth and the Lord taketh away; blessed be the name of the Lord."

Frustrated by Job's noble resignation, Satan ups the ante, savaging Job's body, inflicting boils and running sores from head to foot. Reduced to naked anguish, huddled in a corner, scratching himself with a pot shard, Job still holds his tongue. His wife feels no such compunction. Ridiculing Job's abject piety, she cries out from her own deep pain: "Curse God and die."

Hearing of Job's plight, three learned friends, wise men from the east, journey to visit and comfort him. The sight of his anguish appalls them. They rend their clothes, cover themselves with dust, and sit beside him for a weeklong vigil, consoling him by their very presence. Ironically, only before they attempt to assuage Job's pain by helping him make sense of it do his friends serve his deepest needs. They accomplish this simply by showing up. We should remember that the next time a loved one or friend is reduced to ashes.

What can we do or say? Nothing will take away the pain. Which is one reason we may seek to avoid people who are suffering. Our inability to fix things can be awkward for us, even embarrassing, as we reach for and can never find the right words. Since we can't do anything, we may rationalize doing nothing. But consolation is not nothing. Consolation is being with another in his or her aloneness. Being there at her bedside, telling her we love her, holding her hand. Or across the table from him, listening, hearing him repeat the same story over and over again. Not offering false cheer, telling him it will be better soon, or that time heals everything. Not suggesting that he pull himself together, take a shower, go out and enjoy a movie. Not trying to explain, just consoling him, honoring his pain. In Job's case, nothing could have been more helpful. His friends stood by him.

Yet, the storied patience of Job lasted only one week before he succumbed to his anguish. Thenceforth, the Book of Job is the tale of Job's passion, not his patience. Cursing first not God, but the day he was born (wishing darkness to extinguish it) and the night of his conception (stripping it of every joyous cry), Job prays for death and an end to his pain. "Why should the sufferer be born to see the light?" he cries. "Why is life given to men who find it so bitter?" Having done nothing to earn such disgrace, bereft of every possession, his children dead, his land despoiled, robbed of health and finally hope, Job is reduced to ashes.

Job had not sinned. Even God swore as much. Job followed the divine laws, treated his workers well, fulfilled his duties as a husband and father. The question raised by his story is not merely "Why do bad things happen to good people?" but rather "Why do unbearable, even unconscionable things happen to a person who, above all others, walked blamelessly throughout his days?"

An archetype for all subsequent reflection on human suffering and divine justice, the Book of Job may also be read as the first anti-self-help book. Not only is Job powerless to pull himself up by his own bootstraps, but the explanations his three friends offer to reconcile him to his predicament are profoundly unhelpful, impertinent in both senses of the word.

Eliphaz the Temanite speaks first. He defends God's action and Job's troubles as being, by definition, just. From God's vantage point, all of us receive what we deserve. Yet, though God wounds, "he will bind up; the hands that smite will heal." By this orthodox religious reading, no punishment is arbitrary or unjustified. Job may be blameless, but by being human he participates in our shared impurity. Suffering gives us the opportunity to accept discipline. "Happy is the man whom God rebukes!"

At least Eliphaz exonerates Job from personal culpability for his afflictions. Job's other friends are not so kind. Bildad the Shuhite suggests that if Job indeed is blameless in the face of God, his sons must have sinned against him. According to Bildad, the sins of our children can be visited on their parents. Zophar the Naamathite dismisses Job's protestation of innocence with even less sympathy. Job must be fooling himself or lying, for every divine punishment is a quid pro quo. Clearly guilty of some secret, perhaps monumental sin against the almighty, Job should get straight with God, drop his case, and beg forgiveness.

Far from irrational, in fact wishing only to be helpful, Job's friends apply the rigors of logic to his plight. Since God, by common definition, is all-knowing, all-powerful, and just, a logical explanation can surely be found for Job's afflictions. Job's friends present life as a mathematical equation. Under objective and dispassionate examination, life unfolds with rational exactitude and always checks. To make sense of it, Job need only read the script of his life a little more carefully.

Unleashing a torrent of righteous anger, Job retches in response to this sophistry. He spits on his counselors' so-called friendship. Not only had he done nothing to deserve his God-awful fate, but had they been so cursed, Job would be a better friend to them than they to him. He would not attempt to explain away their suffering, offer legalistic bromides, or wag his head condescendingly in response to their complaints: "I would speak words of encouragement, and then my condolences would flow in streams."

Our sympathies may lie with Job, but the annals of philosophy and theology often echo his friends' logic. Theologians jump through flaming hoops "to justify the ways of God to man," and many philosophers do the same, rationalizing human affliction as a means to some higher end. According to those who believe life must make sense for it to be meaningful, evil and suffering can be rationalized by anyone who truly understands the nature of the cosmos.

Plato wrote that "whatever is permitted to befall a just person, whether poverty or sickness, shall conduce to his good." Would that it were so. Both the liberal religious approach to "salvation by character" and that of Christian Platonists, such as Augustine (who considered evil to be nothing more than the absence of good), entertain a like illusion. Try this reasoning on the victim of a drunken driver. Or on an elderly woman who invests her life savings in a con man's personal account.

Perhaps the most insistently logical defense of God's administration of justice was offered by John Calvin. Calvin viewed everything that happens as a preordained part of God's plan, with ultimate ends justifying intermittent means. The conviction that God plans everything in advance led Calvin to the doctrine of double predestination, which claims that some people are born to be saved and others to be damned. So draconian a dispensation may seem extreme, but Calvin's logic demands it. If God is all-knowing and all-powerful, sees to the end of time and shapes the course of salvation history, then it is impossible for an event to occur by chance. Calvin himself said, "Predestination, by which God adopts some to the hope of life and adjudges others to eternal death, no one, desirous of the credit of piety, dares absolutely to deny." By this reasoning, those who question God's distribution of suffering brand themselves as impious.

Another form of predestation is offered by the Hindus. To me, the most attractive aspect of Hinduism is its non-doctrinal quality. But when it comes to explaining the existence of evil, Hindu teachings abandon the mystical for the rational. Ascribing our sufferings to Karma (or the moral force generated by the sum of a person's actions), Hinduism places the blame or credit for what befalls us in this lifetime on what we have done in a past existence. This explains cases in which suffering seems unrelated or disproportional to one's crime, but it follows a logic similar to Calvin's. Both assume that suffering is just and can be understood rationally.

One needn't suffer Job's afflictions to be placed in a Job-like predicament. One need not even believe in God to become a determinist (one who believes that everything that happens is fated to happen) when tragedy strikes. Every instance of undeserved suffering raises precisely the same question and elicits similar rationalizations. Whenever we ask, "Why did this happen to me?" or "What did I do to deserve this?" we invite Job's friends to pay court. At such times the first anti-self-help book may come in handy, by inoculating us against such well-meant ministrations. For as Job discovered, not from his friends but from God, we cannot explain—or explain away—what lies beyond the power of our comprehension.

The Book of Job hints at two possible answers to the problem of evil, especially as manifest in unjust or arbitrary suffering. The first reduces God's power, the second magnifies it. To begin with, in Job, God is neither omniscient nor omnipotent. God has to ask Satan where Satan has been and what he has been doing. And, then, God is powerless to affect Job's fate, once Satan receives permission to do his mischief. If anything, God is just another bystander as the human drama unfolds below. On the other hand, when Job finally lays his pain squarely on God's doorstep, rings the bell, and screams for an audience, challenging God's decency and character, God counters with a divine reminder of our human ignorance when faced with life's mysteries.

God's initial envoy is a fourth interlocutor, Elihu the Buzite. Elihu, much younger than Job's other friends, apologizes initially for his presumption in choosing to intervene in their argument. Here the paradox is wisdom being offered by a youth. God is in all of us, he says. For Elihu, God surpasses our understanding and cannot be contained within the narrow confines of human judgment. Suffering tempers our pride and therefore brings us closer both to God and one another. "Those who suffer he rescues through suffering, and teaches them by the discipline of affliction." We learn our greatest lessons "on a bed of pain." All we can do is humble ourselves in God's presence and wait for God's word.

Part of this final discourse reflects traditional theology, even the notion raised by Eliphaz that suffering builds character. But the other part adds a new dimension, the inscrutability of God and the peril of human pride. When God himself appears, Job is humbled by God's cosmic greatness. God reduces Job to his rightful status in the scheme of the creation, not as righteous man, but as mere creature. All Job learns, and it is everything, is the saving grace of humility. "What reply can I give thee," Job finally confesses, "I who carry no weight? . . . I have spoken of great things which I have not understood, things too wonderful for me to know . . . Therefore I melt away. I repent in dust and ashes."

Job's submission is troubling to those who cry for justice. And the subsequent reward of a new family and possessions far more abundant than before (likely a later addition to the text) offers as pat and unsatisfying a solution to the problem of injustice as the subsequent development in Christian theology of a heavenly reward to make up for all our earthly suffering. But the affirmation of humility, first in answer to human presumption—especially that of the three friends—and then as a rightful response to the mystery of the creation, does bring Job closer to God.

For both empathy and insight, no interpretation of the Book of Job surpasses William Blake's series of twenty-one engravings published in 1825. Blake casts the interplay between the divine and the human, the heavenly and earthly, in the most intimate terms. Job and God look exactly alike. In Job's face, riddled with pain, one sees God suffering below. In God's face, Job appears, strong and yet compassionate, looking down from above, or reaching out from the whirlwind. Blake himself said that not a line of these etchings was accidental. They stand as a summation of his theology. In Blake's view, suffering does not estrange us from God; it unites us with God. Rather than revealing our sin, in however hidden a form, suffering becomes a medium for redemption.

The American philosopher Josiah Royce suggested that Job's problem remains insoluble so long as we believe, as Job did, that God is a distinct being, an all-powerful and all-knowing judge who stands beyond and lords over this world. In Royce's view, "The answer to Job is: God is not in ultimate essence another being than yourself. He is the Absolute Being. You truly are one with God, part of his life. He is the very soul of your soul. . . . When you suffer, your sufferings are God's sufferings, not the fruit of his neglect, but identically his own personal woe. In you God himself suffers, precisely as you do, and has all your concern in overcoming this grief."

An idealist, Royce understood our suffering as a way to perfect God's life. This conclusion fails to pass what might be called "the Holocaust test." But when coupled with Blake's insight into the Book of Job—that our suffering can bring us closer to God and God closer to us— it does bring meaning to what otherwise contradicts all but the most diabolically logical forms of resolution. Anything that brings God closer to us, also brings us closer to one another. As a sacrament conducive to humility, human suffering diminishes the pride that divides us, from one another and from God.

Even Elie Wiesel, who could no longer believe in God when confronted by the horrors of the holocaust, hints that the only God who might still be worth believing in must either be dead or suffering with us. In his novel, *Night*, a death camp prisoner witnesses the execution of a child. He asks, facetiously and rhetorically, "Where is God now?" In his heart, the narrator answers, "Where is He? Here He is—He is hanging here on this gallows."

> *"What is to be has been already,*
> *but God cares for the persecuted."*
>
> ECCLESIASTES 3:15

During the Holocaust, God was neither reigning in the heavens nor found in the details. If God exists, God was in the Oven. As Dietrich Bonhoeffer, a Christian theologian and pastor, wrote shortly before the Nazis killed him, "We are challenged to participate in the suffering of God at the hands of a Godless world."

If God suffers, we must change what we mean when we use the term God. Job's friends could not think this way. Neither could Calvin nor most Christian theologians. But the bottom line is clear. If God is all-powerful, God could have prevented the Holocaust. To argue that the Holocaust was for the good, even as part of a larger plan, is unconscionable. Just read the text. Anne Frank is Job. So is Dietriech Bonhoeffer. And a myriad more, known and unknown, in this and other Holocausts. With them, we enter the heart of darkness. The question remains: does darkness have a heart?

Viktor Frankl survived the Holocaust. In his book *Man's Search for Meaning*, he reflected on why some people were able to endure living hell. Despite all their pain and tribulation, what separated one group from the other was "the failure of the sufferer to find meaning and a sense of responsibility in his existence." Frankl attributes his own survival to two things: first, a book he wrote on scraps of paper that he kept in his shoes; and second, the hours he spent contemplating the image of his wife, wondering what she might be doing, knowing that she might be dead, as in fact she was. Still she saved him. By moving beyond himself—thinking of her and working on his book—he was able to retain a hint of meaning in his life.

Four decades later, the Jewish editor Jacobo Timerman was persecuted and languished for years in an Argentinean jail in retaliation for his investigative reporting on behalf of the disappeared—people who had been apprehended by the police and disappeared without a trace. In his book *Prisoner Without a Name, Cell Without a Number*, Timerman reports that he couldn't bear to think about his wife because it weakened his will. Yet he too found solace in connection, in his case with a pair of eyes in the cell across from his own. Whether a man or a woman he didn't know, but one night until daybreak, they looked at one another, speaking with their eyes. "Nothing could destroy for me," he wrote, "the mutual immortality created during that night of love and companionship."

Just before he was killed, Bonhoeffer wrote, "For a Christian there is nothing particularly difficult about Christmas in a prison cell." This brave and almost inconceivable statement is illuminated in a prayer he wrote in prison: "Lord Jesus Christ, Thou wast poor and in misery, a captive and forsaken as I am. Thou knowest all man's distress; thou abidest with me when all others have deserted me." He too was not alone.

Frankl, Timerman, and Bonhoeffer discovered the heart in the heart of darkness: shared tears, shared passion, and shared pain.

For those of us who suffer so little by comparison, what does their agony have to do with us? Viktor Frankl suggests one answer. Speaking as one who lost his entire family in the Holocaust and barely survived himself, Frankl possessed the humility and wisdom to observe that though "the size of one's suffering is relative, it still fills one's life like iodine in a cup of water." Everyone's life is tinctured by pain. When our own cup is colored by the iodine of affliction, our lives lose the clarity they may once have possessed. This prompts us to ask the question *why.* Why me? Why this? Why now?

As not only earthquakes but Job and the Holocaust also suggest, whatever our affliction, *why* is the wrong question.

"Share with seven—yes with eight—for you never know what disaster will happen here on earth."

ECCLESIASTES 3:10–11

In the wake of the Holocaust, in the early summer of 1945, a brigade of the British 8th army, each member a volunteer from the Jewish population of Palestine, traveled north through Italy from Taranto. Wearing the Star of David on their uniforms, the soldiers encouraged Jewish refugees and survivors to emerge from their hiding places, listened to their stories, and invited them to emigrate to Palestine. Among these soldiers was the late philosopher of religion Hans Jonas. He tells the story of two Jewish sisters from Trieste, one unmarried, the other a widow, who approached him in the bustling marketplace of Udine.

Five years earlier, fleeing Trieste just ahead of the deportation, the sisters were fortunate to escape with two suitcases full of valuables. They rushed to the railroad station, only to find themselves face to face with an SS security guard who was checking identity papers. Just as they abandoned hope, a railway official silently gestured to them to approach a different gate, temporarily unguarded. Safe on the train, hoping to hide under the cover of anonymity, they traveled to Udine, a city where no one knew them. On arriving, they rented an unfurnished attic room. Two days later a van containing a bed and chairs pulled up in front of their apartment. The Archbishop of Udine somehow had discovered their plight and secretly arranged to provide them with at least the elements of a home.

Since the women were not registered and therefore had no ration cards, they could not purchase food or clothing in the stores. Piece by piece, they bartered their jewelry on the black market in exchange for life's necessities. Soon, with little left for exchange, they traded one of their last valuables for a kilogram of fat, offered at an outrageous price. Later that evening, the black market operator who had swindled them arrived at their door. "Forgive me please," he begged. "I didn't know who you were. I was told later and have come to apologize. From you I will not take money." He returned their money and disappeared into the night.

The sisters told this story to Jonas to explain why they would not leave Udine for Palestine. After all, it was in Udine, a place where they were utter strangers, that history had been rescued from itself, liberated, at least a little, from the tyranny of fear and estrangement generated by the Holocaust. They stayed in Udine because there, amidst the darkest inhumanity, they met others who recognized their pain and succored them.

Not unlike Job, these two women, wealthy, content, living a comfortable life surrounded by friends in the neighborhood where they had been born, were suddenly stripped of their former life, terrorized, uprooted, and cast into a sea of strangers. Though their story had a far happier ending than six million others, no theologian dare justify the destruction of their lives. In itself their pain means nothing. No answer was forthcoming to the question, why me?

Yet they discovered home in the hearts of strangers.

"Plainly no one can discover what the work is that goes on under the sun, or explain why humans should toil to seek yet never discover."

Few speak humbly of humility," wrote the French philosopher Pascal. Maybe that is why the surest guarantor of humility is to be humbled. When stripped of our pride, we can more easily cast it off.

This lesson echoes through John Bunyan's odyssey of a soul, *Pilgrim's Progress.* In one of Bunyan's most intriguing metaphors, it turns out that God has a country house (Bunyan employs this exact term). As in John S. Dunne's parable of the mountain, according to Bunyan, God chose a surprising location for this vacation home: not in the mountains or at the shore but smack in the middle of the Valley of Humiliation, the very place where Bunyan's pilgrim, Christian, and all who would follow him to negotiate their passage toward the Celestial City must triumph over Apollyon, the dragon of pride.

Why does God vacation in this dark and daunting valley? Perhaps because here, more than in any other place, we can fully appreciate God's presence. As Martin Luther wrote, "God is the god of the humble, the miserable, the oppressed, and the desperate, and of those who are brought even to nothing; and his nature is to give sight to the blind, to comfort the broken-hearted, to justify sinners, to save the very desperate and damned." For those of us who believe we deserve sunnier climes, Luther shows no patience. "Now that pernicious and pestilent opinion of man's own righteousness which will not be a sinner, unclean, miserable, and damnable, but righteous and holy, suffereth not God to come to his own natural and proper work."

The image of a God who devotes vacation time to forgiving sinners rather than establishing a rewards ceremony for those who have held to a straight path fits the paradoxical slant of the scriptures, but there is more to Bunyan's insight than this. Until we discover humility, we rank ourselves above our neighbors and have little use for God. According to Jesus (whose words hold power whether we consider him a great teacher, savior, or fellow Jew), love to God and neighbor sums up all the law and the commandments. Humility, which inspires us to kneel before God and next to our neighbor, emerges as an essential virtue. When someone asked Saint Bernard to list the four cardinal virtues, he replied, "Humility, humility, humility, and humility." Even as pride separates us from one another and God, humility breaks down the barriers between us. We become "a part of" rather than "apart from" a common body, the "one body with many members" that Paul describes in his first letter to the church in Corinth.

Reflection on the relationship of the whole to the parts goes back much farther than the first century of our common era. The question of how "the one" relates to "the many," first posed by the pre-Socratic Greek thinker Parmenides, is the cornerstone of Western philosophy. Throughout history philosophers have discovered the essence of life either in the whole or in the parts. For some, an original unity comprehends all the fragments that comprise it. For others, the whole is composed by the myriad parts that construct it. Ancient wisdom teaches that neither can flourish at the expense of the other. For the body to thrive, each member must be honored for its own sake and gifts, the most honor, according to Paul, accorded to those who are least respected. In Paul's metaphor, which he adapted from the Stoics, though the whole takes precedence over the parts, it can flourish only if all of the many are honored and nurtured in their particularity. Yet, to preserve the whole, cooperation must supersede competition. For, where *would* the ear be without the mouth, where the hand without the foot?

There is no higher teaching. "If one member suffers, all suffer together."

"If one should fall, the other helps him up."

As an individual virtue, humility counters pride. Can it function as a social virtue as well, guiding our conduct toward one another? This is harder to imagine, for the societal counterpart of loving one's enemy—turning the other cheek, or giving one's coat and cloak to anyone who asks—appears to invite submission to evil forces as well as good.

We can find one answer by looking at human liberation movements, people devoted to the establishment of justice and equality. Liberation theology is predicated on two principles. First, societal prejudice affects entire groups—such as the poor, women, or ethnic and sexual minorities—not just individuals. Therefore, reformers must advocate for the rights and well-being of the group as a whole. When greater parity of opportunity is fostered, the one body is served.

The second principle of liberation theology is founded directly in humility. Jesus had a preferential commitment to the poor, not only because they are victims of injustice, but because they often cannot afford to be proud. Again, I am not speaking of the pride that brings us together, but the pride that lifts us above and thereby estranges us from others. In Jesus' view, humble people are much more likely to open their hearts to others than prideful people are.

The problem with establishing corporate humility as a social goal is that, in religion as well as politics, we often come together as brothers and sisters only when we lock arms against a common enemy. For this there is only one solution, a paradoxical one. To turn this roadblock to humility into a bridge, we must together discover even larger enemies, enemies that threaten not only some of us, but all.

In the summer of 1993, throughout the Midwest, the common enemy was a flood. "God is making this flood for a reason," one witness said as she watched dozens of people from as far away as Ohio and New Hampshire trying to keep the Mississippi River out of her backyard just north of St. Louis. "It's to make us all come together." However questionable her theology, it is true that whenever natural disaster strikes, people overcome their differences to better struggle against a common foe.

This model can be expanded. In any large American city the real enemies are crime and drugs, bigotry, bureaucracy, and corruption. Each beleaguers every group, regardless of faith, class, or color. Each hurts everyone outside a small criminal or corrupt element that feeds on our body politic like a cancer. If we were to unite to fight these common enemies, all, both individuals and the commonweal, would benefit.

The same is true of internecine hatred. Here, despite the emergence of ancient tribal conflicts in the wake of communism's demise, there are signs of hope. In the Middle East, given the historic animosity between the Israelis and the Palestinians and the seemingly endless cycle of terror, who could have imagined Yasir Arafat and Shimon Peres walking together, holding hands, pledging mutual affection and prophesying peace? This moment, and those that have followed since—even in the tragic wake of Israeli prime minister Yitzhak Rabin's martyrdom—hint that they and many of their people may finally discover a common enemy much larger than one another: war itself.

The question remains, how can we transcend the many temptations to demonize one another, to scapegoat, to attack other members of the one body rather than joining forces against a common enemy? We will only be united when we recognize our own experience of the universal human sacraments—pain and suffering, grief and death—in the lives of others, even our chosen enemies. Death has no respect for persons, races, religions, or ethnic groups. Nothing unites us more profoundly than our common suffering and pain. Our mutual destiny, the dust in which all mingle, is the ultimate proof of our kinship.

In an old parable about the difference between hell and heaven, a group of people with their arms in splints are sitting around a great bowl of soup. Because they cannot bend their elbows, they cannot bring the soup to their own lips. This is hell. Heaven is the same group of people sitting around the same table feeding one another.

In a small town in Israel, a struggling nonsectarian language school suspended classes for three days when a nearby Arab village was flooded by heavy winter rains. The faculty and all the students—Muslims, Christians, and Jews—responded to their neighbors' emergency, working in shifts around the clock to bail the village out. An uncomprehending Israeli minister of education asked the school's director, "What do you think you're doing, when you have your own trouble all around you?"

To which she replied, "What's 'around'?"

"The wise man's heart leads him aright."

ECCLESIASTES 10:2

In the legend of the Holy Grail, the prize sought to guarantee salvation is a cup cut and fashioned from a single emerald stone. Even as communion in Christian churches symbolizes sacramental participation in the body of Christ and vicarious participation in Christ's redemptive suffering, the grail was believed to contain the essence of both Christ's body and Christ's spirit and to satisfy all hunger through the agency of the consecrated host. This image becomes clearer when one learns the secret to securing the grail. In one version of the story, it is guarded by a king who is paralyzed from the neck down. Yet even the greatest warrior in the world cannot wrest the grail away from him by force. Instead, the perfect prize will be given to the one who first asks the guardian of the grail, "What are you going through?"

In September 1993, President Clinton invited forty-six Arab and Israeli boys, ranging in age from eleven to fourteen, to attend the signing of the Israeli-Palestinian peace accord at the White House. These boys had spent the end of the summer together at a camp in Maine in a program called "Seeds for Peace." At the camp, all of the children were matched with buddies from the opposite delegation.

Each boy arrived well acquainted with his own and his people's pain: the loss of grandparents, parents and siblings, victims of everything from the Holocaust to random terror on the West Bank. One early project had the children draw pictures of their buddies and exchange them. One of the Palestinian boys illustrated his picture with hearts, peace signs, and swastikas.

This prompted a crisis. One child, a cousin of Elie Wiesel, cried hysterically. A Palestinian boy couldn't believe that his tears were legitimate. After all, the Israeli was crying for ancestors he had never met, whereas he had lost members of his immediate family. The group broke down in complete chaos. John Wallach, one of the group's advisors, thought the experiment had failed.

He turned out to be wrong. The catharsis of tears, grief, and pain didn't divide these children. It united them. For the first time they saw their own tears in their enemy's eyes. Though it took time, the result was a new sense of kinship. As the Palestinian children prepared to leave Washington, three of them asked to change the final day's agenda so that they could visit the Holocaust museum.

Salvation may be an individual quest, but redemption is a corporate enterprise.

PART IV

In the Middle of the Story:
Lifelines to Hope

"Who can tell a man what will happen under the sun after his time?"

ECCLESIASTES 6:12

On Long Island in the summer of 1995, a sixteen-year-old boy saved his best friend from almost certain death. His friend had been stung by a dozen hornets, and in an allergic reaction, his respiratory system shut down. The young hero carried his friend on his shoulders ten blocks to the emergency room of their local hospital, where paramedics saved the boy's life. Shortly thereafter, the mayor of their hometown hosted a ceremony to honor him. One week later, the friends went out squirrel hunting together. In a freak accident, the young hero shot the boy he had saved in the head, killing him instantly.

As with many true stories, including certain chapters of our own lives, this real-life tale has no apparent moral. Only this perhaps. The plots our lives take can turn without warning. Outside the pages of novels, our life stories seldom end in a tidy, morally coherent manner.

To divert myself while finishing this book I read seventeen Patrick O'Brian novels. For those of you unacquainted with O'Brian's Aubrey/Maturin series, they conjure up the most delicious blend imaginable of Jane Austen, Joseph Conrad, and the Hardy Boys. Each novel is a long chapter in the interlocking lives of two sea-adventuring friends. I didn't let go until the five-thousandth page ran out. Right in the middle of the story.

How frustrating this was: to enter another world (in this case the British naval world during the Napoleonic wars), to have the privilege of sharing these two men's fascinating, difficult, often illuminating lives, their conversation, their dreams, and then to have to wait, prayerfully, in the hope that the author will soon finish the next chapter of their story.

The last book's final words, "Stephen, you must never go to sea anymore," may not strike those of you who have not read seventeen Patrick O'Brian novels as the most poignant sentence in all literature, but I wept when I read them. I couldn't stand letting go. I wanted to open the first page of book eighteen to find out whether Stephen Maturin went to sea again, and if he did, how this affected his marriage, and how he felt about that, and how she felt, and what happened to their daughter. I wanted to know how his life continued, even how it ended, and what he thought and felt right before he died.

That is one of the advantages novels are supposed to

offer: a telling and meaningful finish to the story. Denied that, I actually learned something about what it means to die. When we die, everyone else's story goes on, but we are not there to discover how they turn out.

We know what it is like when others leave. Our parents, friends, heroes. But what about us? When I closed the last page of O'Brian's saga, I experienced what it must be like. For an odd, even eerie, moment, I was gone and they went on. The story continued, as all stories continue: "Yes, I will"; "No, you mustn't"; children and then grandchildren; successes; failures; startling reversals; familiar exchanges; this war and then the next war; "Believe me!"; "I'm sorry." The story continued, but I didn't. They lived on; I died. I stopped, and the eighteenth novel opened without me.

But that's the way it is. Our lives stop in the middle. They don't reach a conclusion, they simply stop. The middle of the story is where all our stories end. As much as I would love to read another Aubrey/Maturin chapter, the possibility that I will not be able to is real. These seventeen books may comprise one seamless, if incomplete, novel, but in a strange way, it is a more realistic novel without an ending, without all the loose ends tied, than if it had one.

I close this book in the same spirit: no loose ends tied, no final conclusions. Only evidence for hope.

In the fall of 1995, I attended my twenty-fifth college reunion at Stanford University. I spent more than a tenth of my life at Stanford, first as a student and then for a year as assistant to the dean of the chapel. Stanford was home to me, a place where I put down roots and found a sense of belonging.

But going home to this old home of mine was completely disorienting. So many new buildings had been erected that I had no sense of bearings. I felt more out of place than I do even when I visit a new city.

And then there was the culture shock. I graduated from Stanford in 1970, at the height of the anti-Vietnam student rebellion. In the spring of 1970 four students at Kent State University were killed protesting the U.S. invasion of Cambodia. In response, we shut Stanford down three months before graduation, spending much of our time at teach-ins and mass demonstrations in White Plaza, right in the center of campus. Twenty-five years later, White Plaza was teeming with activity, hundreds of well-tailored students patiently awaiting their turns to speak with high-tech and financial recruiters at an all-day job fair. This home to which I had returned left me feeling far less like a returning traveler than an extraterrestrial anthropologist who knew so little about what he was seeing that he could make no earthly sense of it.

The following two days I began to find my home. The occasion was the seventy-fifth birthday celebration of my father-in-law, Earle Buck. His wife, Minna, three children and their spouses, and his grandchildren gathered in Napa Valley for a weekend together in his honor. A sense of home emerged in a place where most of us had never been before. This sense of home resonated not from place, but from relationship, the deep, complicated bonds that distinguish every family. We could only revisit it, because everyone around that table had at more than one time and in more than one way moved on. As is often the case, we had fashioned independent thoughts and views, not in imitation of but in reaction to our shared past experience.

Our various homes are not places we return to; we can't. So much of the disappointment we experience when we try to return home stems from a mistaken impression of where home is or ever can be. When I left Stanford twenty-five years ago, I didn't leave my heart in Palo Alto. I took it with me. Any attempt to return home in search of our hearts only leads us away from them.

Yet I did find my heart in the Napa Valley, somewhere I had never been before. Despite an abundance of fruit and grapes, this wasn't Eden. All of us had all long since eaten of the fruit of the tree of the knowledge of good and evil. Each of us had been cast from that garden to which there is no return. There were tensions, arguments, childishness, pettiness, occasional tears. But that's what home is like, not a place, not a cocoon, not an imagined simpler or more innocent site where we flourished before we moved on, before we got lost. This is important to remember. If home is where the heart is, and our hearts are somewhere else—at our original hearth, or college, or anywhere we happen to have moved on from—then we are truly homeless.

One event at my Stanford reunion did touch me deeply. Right before our class dinner, I was honored to read the names of our classmates who had died, so that we could commemorate them with a moment of silence. More than fifty names were on that list. Most were not familiar, but one, my friend Dalton Denton, gave flesh and blood to all the others. As the names rang through the silence, we were one then, our hearts together, our fallen classmates present in the room, and nothing had changed. We were one body, many members, joined in place, returned in time, home again, home where our hearts were.

> *"Better to go to the house of mourning,*
> *than the house of feasting."*
>
> ECCLESIASTES 7:2–3

A woman told me recently of an apparent miracle that took place late one summer afternoon in her New York City apartment. As she sat reading on the couch, a breeze fluttered the curtains and she felt a presence in the room. She looked up from her book and there, directly in front of the window, stood a gentle-faced older woman, her body draped in a diaphanous white gown.

"Who are you?" the young woman asked.

"Don't worry, dear," the figure replied. "Everything is fine."

The telephone rang. Awakened from her reverie, the young woman reached down and picked up the receiver. It was her mother, calling from Ohio. "Sweetheart, Grandma passed away just a few minutes ago." The apparition was gone, but for the moment it didn't matter. So was her grandmother. All she could do was bury her face in her hands and weep.

But now she was in my study. "How can you explain it?" she asked. "Did my grandmother visit me after she died? Was it an angel?"

A growing number of people tell of being visited by angels these days. As far as I can tell, not since the time of the Bible have so many sightings been reported. This young woman's story is one of many I have heard, not only stories of angels, but various other tales from the spirit world, inexplicable encounters with a higher or different reality. I am an agnostic when it comes to angels, but I do believe that untold mysteries abide in the realm beyond our knowing.

The problem with angels is not that angels don't exist. The problem, as with all esoteric religious claims, is that the supporting evidence is not convincing. Even if a world flush with angels looms just beyond the reach of our senses, we can't know it save through our own experience. One person's angel is to another proof only of an overheated imagination. I appreciate the urge to glean meaning from mystery, but I also believe that our desire to master the secrets of creation is wishful thinking. Mystery is not susceptible to the power of logic, only to the reverence of awe. In expressions of awe, the heart honors what the mind cannot comprehend.

I cannot explain what happened in this young woman's apartment. It remains a mystery to both of us. But one thing is certain, a very fine thing. She sat on her couch that midsummer afternoon and wept. Her grandmother had died, and her heart was broken. She could scarcely bear the pain. Talk all you wish about miracles. To me, this young woman's love and suffering suggest more about life's meaning than a supernatural encounter ever could.

"The right happiness of mortals is to eat and drink and be content with all the work they have to do under the sun, during the few days God has given them to live, since this is the lot assigned to them."

ECCLESIASTES 5:17–18

It is tempting to seek meaning not in what we have, but in what we desire. When we do this we practice wishful thinking. Of the enemies that frustrate our search for meaning, this is perhaps the most traitorous. It places fulfillment forever beyond our reach, in what we do not have, in what we cannot do, in who we shall never be. Such fulfillment is at the top of an endless golden staircase. Somewhere high on his climb to nowhere stood J. Paul Getty, the multimillionaire. At the end of his life he cursed his wealth and said he would trade it all for one happy marriage.

The quest for happiness is fraught with such pitfalls. Public people lament their loss of a private life. Millions of unknowns dream of being famous. Beautiful people find reasons to regret their beauty; plain people, their plainness. One man chafes under marital vows. Another mourns the emotional barrenness of one-night stands. One woman, a homemaker, wishes that she were as confident and as successful as her neighbor, a businesswoman. And right next door the very object of her envy envies her the husband and children that she herself sacrificed for a professional career. Just where you think that the grass would surely be green, it may be dying.

I am no longer startled by this. What startles me still, though it no longer should, is precisely the opposite. Often, just where you'd think that the grass would be dying, it is green.

A man is struggling with a gambling addiction. He has been forced to declare bankruptcy. Everything in his life will have to be rebuilt from the ground up. He hasn't gambled for months. His life is filled with hope.

A woman is fired from her job. After spinning for a time in panic, she stops and reflects on what really matters to her. She savors her freedom, reconnects with lost friends, changes her career track, and goes out looking for a job. Her life is born anew.

A woman is dying. She has been given a month to live. She and her children gather around the bed and talk about old times. They watch a movie together on television. They look at family pictures. Their hearts are filled with love.

Adversity doesn't always bring out the best in people, but it can. That is because adversity, not always but sometimes, tends to strip away our illusions. It forces us to work within tightly drawn and well-defined limits. When we do, everything within those limits is heightened. Little things take on a much higher degree of importance. We count as blessings things that at other times we simply take for granted.

None of us can avoid adversity, loss, or failure, but we can choose how we will respond. One person's response to illness might be to equate health with happiness, notwithstanding her taking for granted all those years when she was healthy. Now she knows the real value of health, having lost it. Another person might respond very differently. For the first time in her entire life she might live each day fully, taking special pleasure in common things, savoring her time with loved ones, knowing it to be brief and therefore all the more precious. As eighteenth-century English theologian Jeremy Taylor said after losing all his earthly goods: "I am fallen into the hands of publicans and sequestrators, and they have taken all from me; what now? Let me look about me. They have left me the sun and moon, fire and water, a loving wife, and many friends to pity me and some to relieve me."

We *can* be crippled by grief. Pathological suffering closes us off from others rather than connecting us to them. I am talking about something different: emptying ourselves to be filled, losing ourselves to be found, giving away our hearts even though they surely will be broken. And throughout the days we suffer, remembering that pain, physical or spiritual, can be a sign of healing.

Meaning doesn't emerge from longing for what we lack, things we have lost or will likely never find. The past is over. Pine over it and what we are pining for is probably very different in selective memory than it was in reality.

And longing for something in the future may distract us from our enjoyment of the present. Wishful thinking tends to be both sloppy and sentimental. We should wish to think instead for things closer at hand:

> *The courage to bear up under pain;*
> *the grace to take our successes lightly;*
> *the energy to address tasks that await our doing;*
> *the meaning to be found in giving of ourselves to others;*
> *the liberation that follows when we forgive another;*
> *the comfort to be taken in opening our hearts to another;*
> *the joy to be gained even in the most common endeavor;*
> *the pleasure of one another's company;*
> *the wonder that wells within the simple fact*
> *   of our shared being.*

I call this "thoughtful wishing": wishing for what can be ours, what we can do, who we can be. Unlike wishful thoughts, thoughtful wishes tend to come true.

"Just as you do not know the way of the wind or the mysteries of a woman with child, no more can you know the work of God who is behind it all."

ECCLESIASTES 11:5

Until her death a few months ago, one of my parishioners had been struggling with cancer for twenty years. It was a rare genetically transmitted form of cancer, which she in turn had passed on to two of her three children. She felt guilty about that. All I could think of to say to her was this. Every one of us with children, regardless of his or her genes, gives them two gifts, life and death. Every time a woman gives birth, she gives death. The two are hinged together. Without death, life as we know it could not be.

Much religion refuses to accept death as a fair price for life. I can understand that. Once we are alive, we want to stay alive, to live forever, as if death were an undeserved curse, something unfair, too high a price to pay. That's how I feel too, on my bad days. On my good days, I find this attitude blasphemous, an insult both to the creator and the creation.

We were immortal once. As single-celled organisms replicating ourselves forever, death didn't count. On and on we went, populating ponds, covering rocks with moss, participating usefully but mindlessly in the great immortal muck and sludge that finally gave birth to life and death as we know them. Only with the advent of sexual generation and the creation of the individual did death make its appearance.

Think about it. We were immortal until we became interesting. Our most ancient ancestors were immortal. The ur-paramecium, strangely and distantly pregnant with us, was immortal. So were we until we changed. We were immortal until our parents made love and our mother gave us birth and gave us death.

I don't have the faintest idea what will happen when we die. None of us knows for sure. But if someone were to ask you before you emerged from your mother's womb if there was life after birth, and what this life would be like, how would you have replied? Would you have mentioned birds and rivers, the sun and the moon, children, faith, and hope? Would you have foreseen love and grief, guilt and fear, humility, compassion, shared joy and shared pain? Life is far more amazing than we could ever have predicted, even the most prescient embryo among us. So who is to say what will follow? All I know is this. Before death we are witnesses to at least one miracle, the miracle of life.

"Light is sweet, the eyes of the sun are glad."

ECCLESIASTES 11:7

To put this miracle in perspective, imagine the world as a vast cathedral, the first altar cut from rock and stained with blood and tears. Succeeding generations built, destroyed, and refashioned a myriad of apses and transepts, chapels, meeting halls, confessionals, and burial crypts. The work is never finished; each of us adds our own imperfect offerings. As you look about, notice especially the windows, some translucent, others opaque, none more telling than the stained-glass windows, representational or abstract, each with its own tale illustrating life's meaning. In the cathedral of the world, the windows are where the light shines through. They illuminate our story, the story of life and death.

In any given lifetime, we meditate on the light of meaning through only a few windows. According to the accidents of birth, time, and geography, our scope and attention are limited, focused on one part of a single transept. We do learn from others, but they too are bound by place and, to a lesser extent, by time. Teachers, priests, poets, and scholars pass along new and ancient reflections concerning truth or God.

Some teachers, perceiving the light clearly through their own window, claim that it shines only there, that all other windows give a false view of God's truth. So instructed, religious fanatics may incite their followers to throw rocks through other people's windows. History is rife with terrorists for truth or God. Conversely, we may reject the truth we inherit and search for the light elsewhere.

Sometimes we abandon the search. Observing the bewildering variety of windows and worshippers, we conclude that there is no light. But the windows are not the light, only where the light shines through. We cannot see the light directly, only as refracted. Even as it is impossible to stare at the sun without going blind, we cannot look God in the eye. We can receive illumination indirectly through the windows of creation or as revealed by holy prophets or in sacred writings, but never face to face.

Call God what you will—Yahweh, Allah, ground of being, being itself, creator, oversoul, the holy—God is our name for life's greatest mystery, the power of life with a capital L, or truth with a capital T. What shines through the windows of the cathedral is refracted into millions of glimpses of this Truth, some contradictory, all partial.

In every field of human inquiry, ignorance increases as knowledge grows. The Greek philosopher Socrates once said, "I am the most ignorant man in Athens." He wasn't indulging in false modesty. He was pointing out that others, knowing far less, had no idea how ignorant they were. Socrates's ignorance, the knowledge of how much remained for him to learn, expanded in direct proportion to his learning. Of both belief and knowledge, the same is true for us. When reflecting on several years of contemplation on the origins of the cosmos, one cosmologist sighed, "It's not only queerer than we imagined; it's queerer than can be imagined."

Whether informed by religion or by science, our minds cannot unwrap life's mystery. This is why, in offering evidence to corroborate religious truth, true believers may more honestly be accused of being too rational than too irrational. They are not alone. We all use our minds to figure out things that can't be deciphered by anything as small as our minds. On the other hand, the attempt is a noble one. Trying to decode life's mystery is what makes us human.

Balancing these two apparent contradictions, I base my own theology on contrasting principles: openness and humility. No ceiling limits the expansion of the human heart. Yet, humility teaches that when death visits, we will have attained only a flickering notion of what life and death are all about. The light we discover will be framed by darkness. But, when we ponder the nature of our shared mortality, meaning may begin to emerge. Not unlike when we leave a warm, brightly lit room, go outdoors, and contemplate a dark winter sky: one by one the stars come out.

"A time for peace."

ECCLESIASTES 3:8

Imagine this.

Morning has broken. Our star, the sun, is shining. We are on the beach, gazing at the ocean, tasting the salt air, basking in the sun. Earth, water, air, fire, life's four elements touching. The four elements and us.

"Where did we come from? Who are we? Where are we going?" These are religious questions. The gull doesn't question. Neither does the crab hanging on for dear death from the gull's beak. It is we, at the cross point of the four elements, who watch this drama and ponder.

We do know one thing, where we are. We are on the beach. Several years ago, I read a fascinating book entitled *Powers of Ten*. A series of photographs examines us more closely and then at greater distance. Changing the frame by powers of ten, in one direction we move first from body to hand to knuckle, then to a cluster of hairs, finally reaching the smallest units: cell, atom, and electron. In the other direction, we move from body to a cluster of bodies, then the entire beach, and from there to an expanse of shoreline, a state, half a continent, the globe, on to the solar system, the Milky Way, the universe.

So this is where we are, poised between the infinitesimal and infinitude. In size, we are as many times greater than the smallest of creation's constituent parts as we are smaller than the entire creation itself. Both facts should stagger the imagination of the most committed cynic. According to the latest estimates, the sun is one of fifty to one hundred billion stars in our galaxy. And our galaxy is one of at least fifty billion galaxies. There are as many stars in the heavens as there are grains of sand on almost any beach. And ours is a peripheral star. If the cosmos were a beach, the earth would be a speck of dust on one grain of sand. Yet, on that speck of dust—looking out over the water, air, earth, and fire—we sit, as many times larger than our most submicroscopic part as the universe is larger than we, wondering what it means to be alive and then to die.

That's the easy part, the where part. Who and why, whence and whither, confound us exponentially more. They humble us. Humility reminds us of our smallness: no matter what our minds learn about life, death, God, and the universe, at the end of our lives we still know next to nothing. Openness promises the opposite: the heart places no limit on how much we can learn, change, and love.

Surely we need knowledge gained from honest experience. But our rational minds, whether informed by religion or science, can never resolve the mystery and miracle of life.

When I emerge from a dark passage to find myself reclining on a beach, contemplating the elements, wondering what everything means, I also trust—and every major faith discovers hinted meaning here—the realm of the heart: the place where we meet one another, perhaps even meet the cosmic source for our sense of awe. By overlooking this dimension, cynics and cultured despisers of religion miss almost everything.

Isn't it amazing that we can feel, care and hope, fail and recover, that we often love well, though love is so hard, that we can parcel little parts of ourselves out to others, even touch, speak, and hear? Each is more of a miracle than the parting of the Red Sea or the stopping of the Sun.

Let me make it simple, for it is simple. For us to be here more than a billion billion accidents took place. All our ancestors lived to puberty, coupled, and gave birth. Not just our parents, grandparents, and great-grandparents. Take it all the way back to the beginning, beyond the first Homo sapiens to the ur-paramecium. Even the one in a million sperm's connection with the egg is nothing compared to everything else that happened from the beginning of time until now to make it possible for us to be here.

So how do we respond? Far too often with, "What did I do to deserve this?"

Nothing. Against unimaginable odds, we have been

given something that we didn't deserve at all, the gift of life.

What does this mean? Astoundingly, unbelievably, it means is that we have been in utero from the beginning of the creation. We can trace ourselves back, genetically, to the very beginning of time. The universe was pregnant with us when it was born.

What a luxury we enjoy, wondering what will happen after we die, even what will happen before we die. Having spent billions of years in gestation, present in all that preceded us—fully admitting the pain and difficulty involved in actually being alive, able to feel and suffer, grieve and die—we can only respond in one way: with awe and gratitude.

And how does this affect the way we treat others? I hope it means we will treat others as being as unpredictable, unexpectable, and amazing as we are. In the womb of the universe when God first gave birth, they too have run a billion billion gauntlets, emerging against almost impossible odds to walk here beside us on this planet. They are more than neighbors. They are kin, honest to God and hope to die kin.

Religion does its best (and worst) work here. Not in the creation chapter or the Armageddon chapter, but in the middle of the story, when all the actors are thrown together, struggling for meaning, none knowing as much as we pretend, think, or wish we knew. The wisest of all teachers tells us, "Love God. Love your neighbor as yourself." Even "love your enemy." He instructs us to love our brother, even if he doesn't know that he is our brother.

Love our sister, even if she doesn't know that she is our sister. Exchange pride for humility. Forgive without ceasing. And judge actions but not people, remembering—I would add—that somewhere we and they share at least one common ancestor who, with twenty-twenty hindsight, would do the same for us if she were here.

In fact, she is here. Those who have come before us must now use our hands to touch, our eyes to see. We carry them in our hearts and bones, we and our blood brothers and sisters, survivors of the miracle, of the ongoing mystery, never ceasing to amaze, pouring itself into new vessels, recreating itself, over and over again.

We see little of the road ahead or the sky above. And the dust we raise clouds our eyes, leaving only brief interludes to contemplate the stars. All we can do is stop for a moment and look.

Look. Morning has broken and we are here, you and I, on the beach, breathing the air, feeling the sun, watching and listening to endless waves, digging our toes into the shifting sands.

Dust to dust.

Heart to heart.

Library of Congress Cataloging-in-Publication Data

Church, F. Forrester.
    Life lines: holding on (and letting go) / Forrest Church.
      p. cm.
    Includes bibliographical references (p.).
    ISBN 0-8070-2722-7 (cloth)
    ISBN 0-8070-2723-5 (paper)
    1. Spiritual life—Unitarian Universalist churches. 2. Church, F. Forrester.
I. Title.
BX9855.C48   1996
248.8'6—dc20   96-12620